A DREAM KITCHEN DOESN'T JUST HAPPEN...

- It starts with careful planning.
- It blends beauty with practical working conveniences.
- It suits the size, taste, age and habits of your own family.
- It includes the luxuries you've always wanted—a wall telephone, cook book shelf, recipe file, eating counter, attractive lighting, wipe-it-clean floors, walls and cabinets.
- It is made to order for you—and by you...

With this complete and easy handbook you can turn your recent kitchen into the dream room of your choice or start from scratch with your own remodeling job at a price you can afford.

Here are tips on room shape, appliances, color schemes, storage space, cabinets, counter tops, pass-throughs, decorative touches, everything you want to know.

With do-it-yourself plans, building and installation instructions, and dozens of model kitchens pictured throughout.

ACKNOWLEDGMENTS

We are grateful to the following for photos used in the preparation this book: *Gas Appliance Manufacturers Assn.; Mustchler Bros. Tile Council of America; Frigidaire; Waste King Corp,; Tennessee Stove Works; Marsh Wall Prods.; General Electric; Armstrong Co.; Alsynite; National Gypsum Co,; Dacor Mfg. Co.; Ozite Corp American Plywood Assn.; U.S. Plywood Corp.; Formica Corp.; Owens-Corning Fiberglas; K-Lux Prods.; Artcrest Prods.; Nation Plastic Prods. Co.; Wood Conversion Co.; Westinghouse; Trade Div. of Robbins & Meyers; Nautilus Industries, Inc.; Leigh Prods Inc.; Nutone, Inc.; Majestic Co.; American Gas Assn.; The Mayt Co.; Suter, Hedrich-Blessing; Sears, Roebuck and Co.; Wenczel T Co. and Western Wood Products Association.*

The Family Handyman's
KITCHEN IDEAS

AWARD BOOKS
NEW YORK

TANDEM BOOKS
LONDON

FIRST AWARD PRINTING 1970

Copyright ©1967, 1970 by Universal Publishing and Distributing Corporation

All rights reserved

AWARD BOOKS are published by
Universal Publishing and Distributing Corporation
235 East Forty-fifth Street, New York, N. Y. 10017

TANDEM BOOKS are published by
Universal-Tandem Publishing Company Limited
14 Gloucester Road, London SW7, England

Manufactured in the United States of America

CONTENTS

7	1. A New Kitchen for Your Family
10	Functionalism
14	What Makes a Good Kitchen?
16	Planning
17	The Triangle
19	Appliances
22	Materials and Color
23	Contract or Do-it-yourself
26	Financing the Job
29	Scheduling the Work
30	Eye-catching Idea Kitchens
33	2. A New Ceiling
34	Acoustical Tile
39	An Open-beam Ceiling
41	Install a Suspended Ceiling
43	3. The Walls
44	A Brick Wall—the Easy Way
46	A Vinyl Wall
50	Wipe-clean Wall Paneling
52	Put Your Walls to Work
57	4. The Floor
58	Tiling the Kitchen Floor
63	The Kitchen Carpet
65	5. Electricity in the Modern Kitchen
66	Basics of Good Lighting
72	A Kitchen Ventilation System
73	A Custom-built Range Hood
76	Let's Have a Barbecue

79	**6. Cabinets**
80	Kitchen Cabinet Construction
84	Assemble-it-Yourself Cabinets
90	Kitchen Corner Cabinets
94	Get Yourself Organized
98	Let Lazy Susan Do the Work
100	Special Storage Ideas
105	**7. Countertops**
106	A Vinyl Working Surface
110	Vinyl Surface—the Easy Way
112	A Mosaic Tile Top
114	Plastic Laminate Surfaces
116	A New Counter
123	**8. Laundries**
124	Plan a Kitchen Laundry Center
136	Folding Doors to Conceal a Laundry Center
137	**9. Closets**
138	More Use from Your Closets
142	Closet on a Door
144	Utility Closet
147	**10. A Kitchen You'll Love to Live In**
148	The Planning
158	The How-to
189	**11. What It's Called and Where to Buy it**

1 A NEW KITCHEN FOR YOUR FAMILY

- Functionalism
- What Makes a Good Kitchen
- Planning
- The Triangle
- Appliances
- Materials and Color
- Contract or Do-It-Yourself?
- Financing the Job
- Scheduling the Work
- Eye-Catching Idea Kitchens

Ask any homemaker who's lived with her kitchen for more than a few weeks if she's satisfied with it completely. Chances are she'll have some pretty strong ideas on what can be done to improve it—whether it's a vintage type dating back to the turn of the century or a modern spic-and-span version in a room she designed herself, she can probably now suggest some improvements, for the kitchen is basically a working area, and new ideas for making kitchen work easier and more efficient are constantly popping up—worksaving appliances, and worksaving innovations thought up by the homemaker herself as she uses the kitchen.

So you want to remodel your kitchen because of age, or inefficient layout, or insufficient size, or as part of a general home expansion. Whatever your particular situation, this book is for you. It will cover the basics of good planning—essential to a satisfactory result—and include

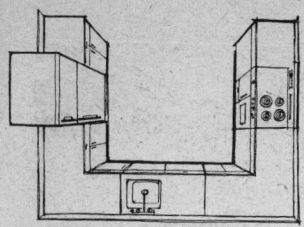

GOOD KITCHENS DON'T JUST HAPPEN

The traffic pattern in the U-shaped kitchen will be a triangle running from the two wings to the center, which is usually the preparation area.

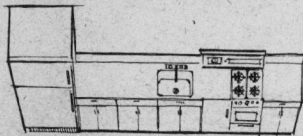

The one-wall kitchen forms a straight line and the sequence outlined above should be followed, windows and doors permitting. The most common errors are the lack of counter space for storage area and serving space from the range area.

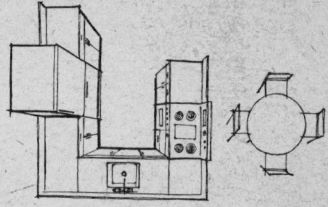

A popular concept found in more modern houses is a version of the U in which one leg is free-standing as an island. This often combines the function of serving the clean-up when the sink is located here. Or the range can be built-in to include serving space for an adjacent informal dining area. The island can double as a snack-breakfast bar, a very desirable feature.

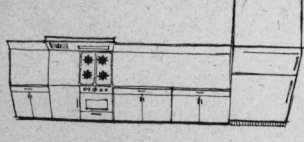

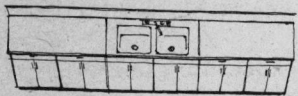

The two lines of a corridor plan should be divided as equally as possible to limit the amount of crisscrossing that is inherent in this layout.

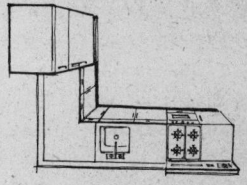

The most common layout is the L-shape, which has some of the merits of the U, but the placement of the utilities is often controlled by windows and doors on the two walls. Wall-hung or under-the-counter refrigerators are very often a workable solution.

a wide variety of projects that you can adopt or adapt to your own kitchen project.

Before you settle down to serious planning, spread the word around the family, give them a little time to think about it, then call a brainstorming session to get all their ideas down on paper (retaining veto power for yourself, of course). Most of these ideas will probably by discarded outright or altered considerably to fit the overall plan. But from them will come a synthesis of what your kitchen should be for your family. Combined with the requirements of the homemaker around whom the kitchen is to be built, and the practical considerations outlined in this article, they will provide the basis of your kitchen planning.

WHAT ARE THE FUNCTIONS OF A KITCHEN?

Certain functions of a kitchen will apply to all families in every situation. The kitchen is a place for preparation of meals, and for cleaning up afterward. It is a work center. It should include storage space for the foods and materials and tools that are used in food preparation—a refrigerator for storing perishables, shelves and cabinets for canned goods and spices, etc., cupboards to store at least those utensils and dishes that are used in meal preparation, as well as those items used in cleaning up (detergents, steel wool pads and the like).

Meal preparation generally centers around the range, but requires in addition a sufficient amount of counter space for cutting, chopping, peeling, combining, or what have you, of the assorted foods under preparation. Lack of adequate counter space is one of the most common complaints housewives mention regarding their present kitchens.

An area of kitchen activity during both preparation and cleanup is the sink. It should be convenient to all other main areas of basic kitchen activity. The sink is the center of the well-known kitchen work triangle, which will be explored in detail later in this article.

Island counter in this kitchen adds a special working surface in the middle of the U design and adds greatly to its utility. Arrangement includes wall display space for your collection of plates, china.

This, then, is the minimum kitchen—meal preparation and cleanup. In reality, of course, the kitchen serves many, many other functions.

For one thing, kitchen storage almost always goes beyond the basic requirements of those things needed to prepare a meal and clean up afterward. Serving dishes—at least those of the everyday variety—are usually found here, as are extra supplies of canned goods, etc.

A number of studies made in recent years have confirmed the fact that housewives have a strong preference for kitchens that include dining facilities—almost always provided in the "good old days" of spacious Victorian-era houses, but often overlooked in the tremendous spurt of construction of the post-war years.

An extension of this is the new/old concept of the kitchen as a general family gathering place. By necessity the pattern during pioneering days—when it was the only communal room in the house, or at least the only heated one—and again popular as the center of many family activities in the era around the turn of the century, the kitchen again emerges in this function as the popularity of open planning in home design persists.

Factors behind this are economic, structural and social. The cost of living space is high, thus it's sensible to double the function of every available cubic foot. The open-planned kitchen, designed not as a walled-in room for pots and pans but as an integrated, family-wide part of the home, pays its high-cost space premium handsomely. Secondly, improved building methods and materials make open planning structurally practical. Formerly, joists had to be erected, evenly spaced, on load-bearing partitions. Today's roof sections are lighter, and effective long-span joists and trusses forego the need for load-bearing partitions. All this means for the modern kitchen is that open planning is possible, regardless of the size of the home.

Modern kitchen ventilating equipment is another important factor in such planning. Without a good range hood-fan unit, cooking odors would drift freely through the open planned house. And with the modern and handsome appliances that are used in today's kitchen, there's little "kitchen drudgery" to be mercifully hidden from the eyes of the rest of the family or guests. When the modern family entertains, the homemaker is a part of the party even as she prepares the meal or refreshments in her open-plan kitchen.

Still another function often assumed by the modern kitchen is that of laundry center. The new laundry appliances no longer make it necessary to hide this function in the basement alongside large stationary tubs. Located in the kitchen or in some other central location, the laundry

Many housewives prefer to have the sink located beneath a window, as shown in the kitchen above. Both kitchens shown here have cooking surfaces set in peninsula counters, built extra wide so passersby will easily avoid bumping utensils on the range.

center allows the homemaker to do the washing incidental to other regular chores, and also to keep an eye on the children during the process.

The modern kitchen also may serve as the housewife's "office," with a small desk and chair, the indispensable telephone and shelves for cookbooks, PTA lists, files for bills and receipts and the like. Here the homemaker plans meals, makes out shopping lists, balances the family budget, makes phone contacts for the community organizations and drives in which she may be involved, and performs any number of other similar chores.

WHAT MAKES A GOOD KITCHEN?

The integrating of all the functions your family wants it to serve, and in such a way that no such function interferes with any other. Particularly it must be remembered that the basic function of the kitchen is preparing-serving-cleaning up of meals. None of its other functions must impair the efficient performance of this basic one. Here is where careful and thoughtful planning enters the picture.

Good kitchens don't just happen. They start with careful planning to blend the ideal in attractiveness with practical working principles. Size of family, ages, activities, working and eating habits, availability of help, even the physical characteristics of the principal users of the room all have a bearing on planning a kitchen that's right for the individual family.

A good starting point in your planning is to list the things that please or annoy you about your present kitchen. This will remind you of what to include or avoid in the new plan. List all the kitchen activities. Note items you may not have now but will want to include, such as a wall telephone, planning desk, shelf for cookbooks and recipe file, an oversized wastepaper basket, a serving cart, a spot for an easy or rocking chair.

Check the many pictures of model kitchens shown

throughout this book and mark those whose arrangements and decorating schemes particularly appeal to you. These will help to form your own thoughts on what is right for you.

How many in your family will be using the kitchen at one time? Do you bake frequently? Do you frequently entertain large groups? Are children at play supervised from the kitchen? Take all these factors into your preplanning considerations.

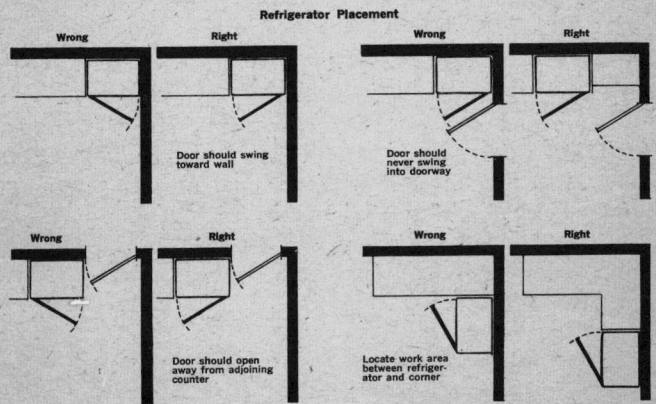

In proper refrigerator placement the door should swing toward wall and never into a doorway, as shown in the two right and wrong illustrations at top. Door should also open away from adjoining counter and work area between refrigerator and corner should be accessible.

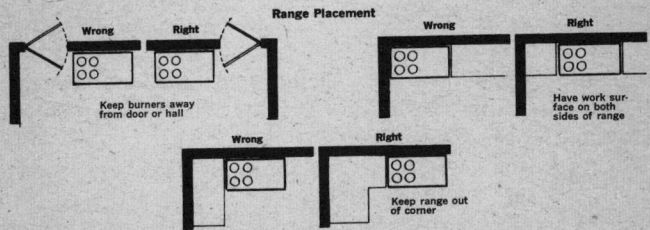

PLANNING

Carefully measure the room and make a scale floor plan, either on graph paper or marking out your own paper on a scale of ½-inch or 1 inch to the foot. Accurately measure and note the locations of windows and door openings. If you are considering moving a wall or eliminating or relocating a door or window opening, indicate the necessary measurements on your plan. On the margin of the plan, note floor to ceiling heights and floor to window sill heights. Also include the exact locations of permanent fixtures such as radiators, pipes and electrical outlets.

On a separate piece of paper, make rough layout sketches, then transfer these experimental layouts to the scale plan. You can either place a piece of tracing paper over the plan, or cut paper or cardboard blocks to scale to represent appliances and cabinets. This allows you to shift them about until you hit the right arrangement for your purposes.

Stock base cabinets are 36 inches high, 24 to 25 inches deep and from 12 to 48 inches wide. Wall cabinets are from 12 to 14 inches high, usually 13 inches deep, and in 12 to 48 inch widths. Dealers' catalogs will give you the exact specifications and also show the various special cabinet arrangements available.

If you plan to build your own cabinets, of course, the dimensions are much more flexible. You might, for example, wish to establish a higher or lower cabinet height to accommodate a very tall or very short homemaker. As long as the kitchen remodeling is for the convenience of *your* family, there is no reason why you should not tailor it to fit. A difference of a few inches either way in counter height is not likely to have any great effect on your home's resale value.

Investigate the appliances available, if your remodeling project is to include new appliances. Find out the exact measurements of the refrigerator or range you will purchase before you go too far in your planning. This can save headaches later on.

A modification of the two-wall layout, the kitchen shown above features a well-arranged, well-defined working area and snack bar.

THE TRIANGLE

As a basic key to their designs, kitchen designers generally use the sink-refrigerator-range triangle. Some general guidelines about the triangle will help you in planning your kitchen.

The sink should be considered the center point of the triangle. The total of the three sides of the triangle should not be more than 22 feet nor less than 12 feet, according to the generally accepted standards of kitchen efficiency. The most trafficked leg of the triangle is that between the sink and the range. Therefore, this would ideally be the shortest leg of the triangle—perhaps 4 to 6 feet. The next most heavily traveled route is between refrigerator and sink; this leg of the triangle might be from 4 to 7 feet. In planning your kitchen around the triangle, try to prevent the normal traffic lanes of the home from crossing the triangle, thus cutting down on the plan's efficiency. Following are the the four basic plans of kitchen layout, based on the triangle concept mentioned above.

1. The U-shaped kitchen is potentially the most efficient of the kitchen plans. The problem of criss-crossing traffic is eliminated since the U is enclosed on three sides. It's easiest to arrange a balanced, efficient work triangle in this layout. Storage space is plentiful, and the corner areas can be utilized with a lazy susan type of arrangement. If your present kitchen is too large to take advantage of the step-saving features of the U kitchen, you can divide the room with one leg of the U, making half the area a work space, the remainder a dining area.

2. The L-shaped kitchen is another functional design, generally allowing more adequate eating area in most layouts. Traffic is kept to one side, away from the work triangle, but it may interfere with the serving path between work area and dining area. Storage is generally less plentiful and less convenient than with the U.

3. The two-wall kitchen is good for small areas, and has many of the advantages of the U. The main drawback is that it is almost always built around a busy thoroughfare from one section of the house to another or to outdoors, thus greatly cutting down the efficiency of the work triangle. If the area can be dead-ended, that solves the problem. The corridor of the two-wall plan should be a minimum of 48 inches, with 54 inches a more comfortable figure.

4. The one-wall kitchen is convenient for use in very tight situations, but counter and storage space are generally sacrificed in order to cram in the necessary appliances and a limited amount of space between them. Resort to this only if there is no other workable solution.

Variations of these plans employ islands and peninsulas to complete the basic work triangle and, generally, enjoy the same advantages and disadvantages of the basic plan to which they are most closely related.

APPLIANCES

If you are undertaking a major kitchen remodeling, you will probably plan to purchase new appliances as part of the project. Take a trip to an appliance dealer's showroom to see the latest models. If you've been using the same range and refrigerator for 8 or 10 years, the new models will amaze you with the many modern features and conveniences that they offer.

Ranges and ovens. You have several styles from which to choose. The high eye-level range with single or double oven, the compact one-piece slide-in, the separate built-in wall oven and counter surface cooking units, and the freestanding models. Decide on the type and size you want, and see how it fits into your overall kitchen plan.

Many homemakers like the separate wall oven and surface units. While these take up a little more space, it's a

Don't be afraid to blend materials in your kitchen. Above, fieldstone, wood, metal and tile make an arresting and handsome combination.

convenient working height. And, since the oven is not used as frequently as the surface unit, placing it a few steps outside of the basic triangle does not destroy the efficiency of the plan.

A double oven range is most convenient for the homemaker who likes to fuss over large meals. She can broil or roast an entree at one temperature while at the same time baking bread or a tempting dessert at another.

Barbecue grilles. Outdoor cookery has become so popular that the barbecue grille has inevitably moved indoors, allowing the devotee of charcoal-broiled steak to enjoy this succulent treat the year-round. Drop-in models are available, using charcoal, gas or electricity for fuel. Also popular are portable models which may be used indoors or out, depending on whim, weather or occasion. Whichever type is used, adequate venting is a necessity. This is usually provided by an exhaust fan inside a hood directly over and slightly larger than the grille unit.

Refrigerator-freezers. You'll be able to fit a large refrigerator with modern insulation into the same floor space that formerly was required for a much smaller model. Be sure to specify right- or left-hand door opening, depending on which way you want the refrigerator door to swing open. You'll probably want a two-door refrigerator with a separate zero-temperature freezer across the top or bottom or at the side. For a large family, you might prefer a matching pair—one that's all refrigerator and another that's all freezer.

Most modern refrigerators require infrequent or no defrosting. Many offer large ice cube storage bins with ice-making devices to keep you in constant supply. Pullout or swing-out shelves bring all food out to you, making storage a cinch. Some models even roll out or ride out on a cushion of air to make cleaning easier. When you choose the refrigerator-freezer for your kitchen project, check on its features and choose a size big enough for present and foreseeable future needs.

This well-planned U-layout includes good working counter space, convenient counters adjacent to refrigerator, range, sink and wall oven. A small office area is conveniently located for supervision.

Dishwashers. Here's a time- and labor-saver that your new kitchen shouldn't be without. As long as you are planning a major remodeling, an undercounter unit is your best choice. If your budget won't take it now, allow space in a 24-inch base cabinet for a future dishwasher purchase. Or, if you can't fit a dishwasher into your present plan, you might consider a portable model where no permanent plumbing or wiring are required. Convertible types can even be built in at a later date.

When planning your dishwasher installation, keep in mind that most right-handed women find it convenient to have the dishwasher on the left-hand side of the sink, and vice versa.

Sinks come in many sizes with single, double or triple bowls of porcelain or stainless steel. Most homemakers prefer the double-bowl variety. When you're thinking about a sink, consider also a food-waste disposer. It's another great labor-saving device.

MATERIALS AND COLOR

How about the materials you use in your kitchen remodeling? Important qualities are durability and easy cleaning. Plastic laminates, vinyls, prefinished cabinet woods, plastic-coated hardboard are among the favorites. Ceramic tile can be used to good effect for countertops and backsplashes, providing a practical as well as colorful touch. The use of various materials for floors, walls, ceiling, countertops and cabinets is covered elsewhere in these pages.

From a decorative point of view, color is a most important consideration, and should figure into the early planning stages. You may wish to include colored appliances in your kitchen, and you will want to coordinate these with the overall color scheme—the walls, wall paneling if it is used, the material on countertops and backsplashes, the cabinets, whether of metal or wood, the flooring.

Dark colors will make the room appear smaller. If an accent wall features fairly dark paneling, or if you have dark wood cabinets, you'd better use white, light yellow or pale green for the remaining walls, white for the ceiling, and a light, lively pattern for the floor.

Light colors make a room appear larger. Blues and greens give a cool feeling, oranges and reds a feeling of warmth. You'd be wise to avoid a color scheme that depends too much on contrast for its effect. Since this room is basically a work area, and one in which a good deal of time is spent, you don't want the color scheme to have a distracting or tiring influence.

CONTRACT OR DO-IT-YOURSELF?

You may not want to undertake the kitchen remodeling job yourself. Perhaps you doubt your ability to tackle such an ambitious project, or maybe your schedule just doesn't allow enough free time for this added work load. There are plenty of contractors around who will be willing to do it, but how do you know you are selecting a reliable one?

The recommendations of friends and neighbors who have been well satisfied with work performed by a contractor are helpful. Your building supply dealer may be able to suggest some reputable firms. A check with your local Better Business Bureau before you make a final selection will be available in determining whether others in

One-wall kitchen sacrifices counter area to fit in appliances. In this case dining area is gained. Unit at right adds some storage space. Use the one-wall plan only when no good alternative exists.

your community have complained of trouble with a given contractor.

You should get at least three estimates on the job, and make sure that each contractor's bid includes use of the same quality materials, and guarantees the same amount of work to be done. No matter how much trust you may place in the contractor you finally select, insist on a written contract for the job.

The contract should specifically indicate the work to be performed, how it will be done and how you will pay for it. It should provide a method of determining extra charges for any changes that you request during the progress of the work. This is important to protect you from excessive extra charges, and a responsible contractor will also want to protect himself from losses through work having to be redone, and from misunderstanding and ill will through no fault of his own.

The contract should call for the contractor to obtain any needed permits and see to any necessary inspections and certificates as the work progresses. It should also provide that the contractor be insured, as required by law, for workmen's compensation and for personal injury and property damage. And you may wish to ask for a completion bond, paid for by the contractor, to protect you in the event that he is unable for any reason to finish the job. Finally, specify in the contract that any debris from the job be hauled away by the contractor.

Find out when the contractor will start the job, and how long it will take him to complete it. If you are dealing with more than one contractor, you will have to coordinate their services. After the carpenter has framed the walls and partitions, for example, the electrician and the plumber will have to be called in to do their roughing-in before the wall material is applied.

Regarding payments to the contractor, make it a rule never to give any money for any home improvement project in advance. On a fairly large job, as where a kitchen

In this layout a snack bar has been included by locating the range in a cabinet away from the wall. However, major traffic patterns of the home pass directly through the work triangle, uninterrupted.

is being relocated in a new wing of the home, the contractor will want partial payments during the course of the work—for example, a third when the job is half completed, another third on completion, and the balance when all necessary certificates are obtained. Some homeowners want the right to withhold a part of the payment for a period of time, usually two to three months, to give them a chance to "live with" the job and make sure that everything is satisfactory.

Many handyman homeowners prefer to have a contractor do part of the job while supplying the finishing touches themselves. You may wish to have a professional do all the roughing-in—furring the walls, framing partitions, etc.—

and then install the paneling, ceiling tiles and floor yourself. Or you may have the carpenter finish the walls, then take over to make the built-in cabinets and other refinements.

In any event, you will probably have such tasks as plumbing and electrical work professionally done. Perhaps you can work along with these tradesmen if you so choose—boring holes and pulling wires for the electrician while he makes the connections and installs the fixtures, or doing the relatively simple connecting of new water supply lines into existing lines, while leaving the more complex work of connecting waste and vent lines to the professional plumber.

Whatever you decide to do, make sure that all the agreed-upon conditions are clearly spelled out in the contracts that you draw up with the various tradesmen, so that there can be no misunderstanding about who is responsible for what. And see that you live up to your end of the agreement, doing whatever must be done in good time so that you don't cause unnecessary delays for the contractors. Time is money to them, and if they are forced to wait for you to do your job, it's cash out of their pockets. You can be sure they won't be so willing to work along with you next time you undertake a home improvement project.

FINANCING THE JOB

Whether you agree to a contractor's bid on your project or whether you estimate material requirements and determine the cost of doing it yourself, you must know how much money it will take to do the job. The next question is how you are going to pay for it. Chances are that you'll finance it. And you'll probably find lending institutions in your locale more than happy to finance your kitchen improvement, for they consider such a loan a solid investment.

There are many types of credit organizations that are in business to help you finance your projects (and, of course, to make a reasonable profit along the way). Once you have determined how much you will need for the project, shop around to find the one that best suits your requirements.

For a relatively small amount—say a few hundred dollars—you can secure a personal loan from a bank or a loan from a consumer finance company. The former usually has more rigid credit requirements, but if you can meet them, the loan is generally easy to come by. Maximum amount will depend on your salary and financial obligations, as well as the availability of credit in the area

Although designed for a limited area, this kitchen includes many desirable features—good counter space, a snack bar, ample storage, corner sink, counter space adjacent to appliances, good work triangle.

in which you live. Repayment is usually required in three years or less, and the cost is computed either as a discount (you receive less than you actually borrow) or an add-on rate (you receive the full amount, but you repay a greater amount).

For a loan from a finance company, you will probably pay somewhat more than for a bank loan, but the money is usually easier to get. How much you can borrow and the rate of interest you will pay differ from state to state.

A popular financing method for fairly large home improvement projects is to add the cost of the project to an existing mortgage—if it has an open-end clause. This clause allows the mortgagee to reborrow the difference between what has already been paid off and the original amount, at the original rate of interest. The usual arrangement for repayment is to increase the regular mortgage payments. This eases the payment problem if a substantial amount is borrowed. But if it is only a small amount, this type of financing is somewhat impractical, particularly if the mortgage still has a long period to run, as the interest over such a period would be considerable. The bank will probably require detailed estimates and plans of the work that is to be done when you apply for this type of loan.

The Federal Housing Administration's Title I program insures home improvement loans made through banks up to a maximum of $3500. All you need to qualify are a loan application and a signed estimate from your contractor. If you want to do the job yourself, you'll need a bid from a building supply house for the materials you'll use. Credit rules are as strict as for other bank financing. The advantage of this type of loan is the low discount rate that the bank is allowed to charge.

If you qualify under FHA's 203K program, you may borrow up to $10,000 for home improvements, and spread your payments up to 20 years at a simple interest rate of 6% plus ½% for FHA insurance. The minimum loan is

$2500 ($1000 in urban renewal areas). The amount you can borrow is, of course, dependent on your income, credit rating, and the value of your property. The advantage is obvious—it allows you to set up a repayment program tailored to your situation.

SCHEDULING THE WORK

In most kitchen remodeling projects, you will have to live with the work as it progresses. Some fortunate few may have auxiliary kitchens in their basements that can be used during the remodeling; others may even be able to move out of the house—to a summer cottage, for example—while the work is being done. But most of us will just have to grin and bear the inconvenience. However, you can stage the work to make the inconvenience as slight as possible.

Discuss this with the contractor or subcontractors before the work begins. Plan the job so that the essential fixtures and appliances—sink, range, refrigerator—can be removed and replaced in the least possible time. With a bit of careful planning and cooperation on the part of all concerned, there's no reason why the job can't be accomplished with a minimum of difficulty for tradesman, do-it-yourselfer and homemaker. Before you know it you'll be the proud possessor of a spanking new kitchen.

With careful planning and intelligent cooperation on the part of your contractor or whomever you may enlist, you don't have to put limits on your imagination.

EYE-CATCHING IDEA KITCHENS

The modern kitchen in Oriental motif shown on the following page may seem a bit "far out" for your modernization project, but it illustrates the fact that, in planning the modern kitchen you can give free rein to your sense of

design and even indulge in your personal tastes in the room's theme.

Actually, the gleaming white appliances and cooking unit set into a slab in the middle of the room are an appropriate implement to begin the wood paneling, bamboo and driftwood arrangements and traditional Far Eastern designs, while modern in function.

Less exotic but no less pleasant a place in which to live and work is the remodeled kitchen illustrated at left on the following page. In this large room the homeowner

utilized a raised cabinet and a hanging unit to separate a rear entryway.

Another use of a cabinet as a divider is seen at right, above. Here the cabinet with its surface cooking unit is built out at an angle to the wall to provide plenty of working space on the kitchen side.

A circular, table-height snack bar—the telephone enables it to double as a comfortable conversation corner—is on the other side of the divider.

The basic rules of cabinet construction are illustrated in the section of the book under that heading. Various specialized cabinets are shown elsewhere in the book—see: Put Your Walls To Work.

2 A NEW CEILING

- **Acoustical Tile**
- **Open-Beam Ceilings**
- **Suspended Ceiling**

ACOUSTICAL TILE

Ceiling in rough shape? You'll certainly want to include a new ceiling as part of your kitchen remodeling project.

Even if your present ceiling is free of bad cracks or breaks, there are several reasons why you might want to replace it. For one, the kitchen is generally the noisiest room in the home. A ceiling of acoustical tile will greatly reduce the noise within the room, absorbing and thereby eliminating up to 70% of the excess sound that strikes it. Sound enters the small holes in the surface of the tile and the sound energy waves are trapped when they strike against the tile's porous fibers.

Another kitchen problem that might be solved by a new ceiling is that of a room which seems visually unbalanced because the ceiling is too high in proportion to the floor area of the room. Here, a suspended ceiling is in order. This type of ceiling also allows full, overall illumination of the kitchen, if you install fluorescent fixtures above and use the translucent ceiling panels offered by a number of manufacturers.

Or perhaps it is simply a matter of decor. If you are remodeling the room into a "colonial kitchen," you will probably want a simulated open-beam ceiling to complete the effect. You can build a false beam of wood, but there are several more simple ways to do it. There are even simulated wood beams for use with suspended ceiling systems.

On this and the following pages are shown typical installations of various ceiling materials.

Where the existing ceiling is basically sound, even though there may be cracks, acoustical tiles may be cemented right over it, as shown on preceding page.

Where the ceiling is in bad shape (photos above), furring strips may be nailed over it, or the old ceiling may be removed and the furring nailed to the joists.

The first furring strip is nailed along the wall. The placement of the second strip depends on the width of the border tiles to be used.

Carefully check the levelness of the furring strips, using a straightedge and carpenter's level, to insure firmly anchored tiles and an even ceiling. Shim where necessary to fill out low spots as shown in top photo.

Measure the area to be covered to determine the width of the border tiles and when all furring strips are in place and properly leveled, snap a chalk line (photo above) across them to mark the position of the border tiles. Follow the same procedure along all four walls before beginning tile installation.

Each border tile must be measured precisely and cut individually to ensure accurate fit. Cut the tile face up, using a coping saw or a sharp knife, as shown in the top photo. A jigsaw knife blade may speed up the work if power tools are available.

Start your tile installation in a corner of the room. Cut the first tile to fit the chalk-line intersections and staple the tile into position as shown in the lower photo. Attach border tiles along each wall outward from the corner.

Work out installation across the ceiling, filling in with full tiles after placing the border tiles, as illustrated in the photo above.

An excellent idea is to predetermine as closely as possible the exact location of the ceiling fixtures as the work progresses. Wherever possible these should be positioned in the center of a tile to minimize fitting. See lower photo. Adjust the ceiling fixtures to be flush with the face of the tile. Border tiles at the opposite wall are face nailed to complete your new ceiling.

AN OPEN-BEAM CEILING IN SIX EASY STEPS

To create dramatic open-beam ceilings is easy, using simulated wood beams that simply fold into shape as illustrated above. The hardboard beams are vinyl-surfaced, predecorated in deep-textured walnut pattern and come in flat lengths of 12, 14 and 16 feet. The board is folded along precut grooves running lengthwise to form a beam 4" deep and 2 1/3" wide. For extra rigidity, run a bead of glue along each groove before folding.

The six simple steps of installation are shown on the following page. The first is to nail 1x3 furring strips to the ceiling at desired intervals—top left photo. Next fit the folded beam over the furring strip, snug to the ceiling (top right and following photo) and nail through the hardboard from each side into the furring strip.

For the corner starting beam, one side of the beam is cut away and an extra furring strip is nailed to the wall, as shown in upper sketch. Note measurements carefully. Lower sketch shows finished starting beam.

The beams can be made to serve a utilitarian function as housing for electric conduits. Several decorating arrangements are possible—beams can be run parallel or used to form an intersecting design.

Lightweight and easy to handle, the beams can be cut to shape with a crosscut saw to fit existing moldings. Durable vinyl covering offers maintenance-free service.

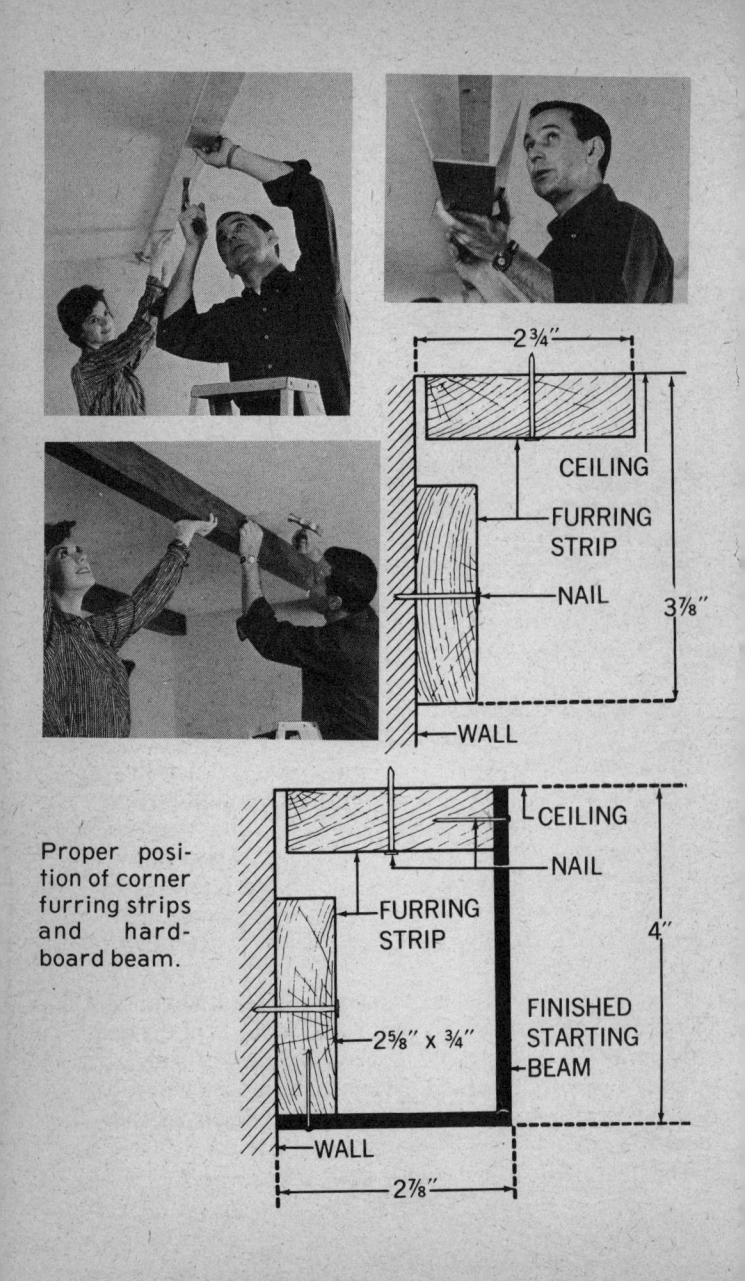

Proper position of corner furring strips and hardboard beam.

Diagram 1 labels: 2 3/4", CEILING, FURRING STRIP, NAIL, WALL, 3 7/8"

Diagram 2 labels: CEILING, NAIL, FURRING STRIP, 2 5/8" x 3/4", WALL, 2 7/8", 4", FINISHED STARTING BEAM

INSTALL A SUSPENDED CEILING

Despite the modernization project in the kitchen shown above, which included the installation of new cabinets and appliances, the room seems visually ill-proportioned because of an old-fashioned high ceiling. A suspended ceiling can be easily installed, as shown on the following pages, using either solid panels or translucent ones for a fully luminous ceiling.

The first step in installation is shown in the top left photo, next page. Fasten wall angles around the perimeter of the room at the desired new ceiling height, leveling as you go. T-rails are rested on the wall angles and wire hangers are threaded through holes drilled in the T-rails and are attached to the ceiling for support, as shown in the illustration at top right. Wires may be attached to the existing ceiling with nails or screw eyes and are required at every four feet along the main rails and on each side of all splices.

Cross T-rails are attached between the longitudinal rails. The ends of the cross rails rest on the channels of the main rails, middle left photo. Distance between rails is dictated by size of panels you select. Standard sizes are one or two-foot squares. Place panels in the T-rail channels, as shown in middle right photo. Tilt and drop into place.

The final effect is shown in the bottom picture.

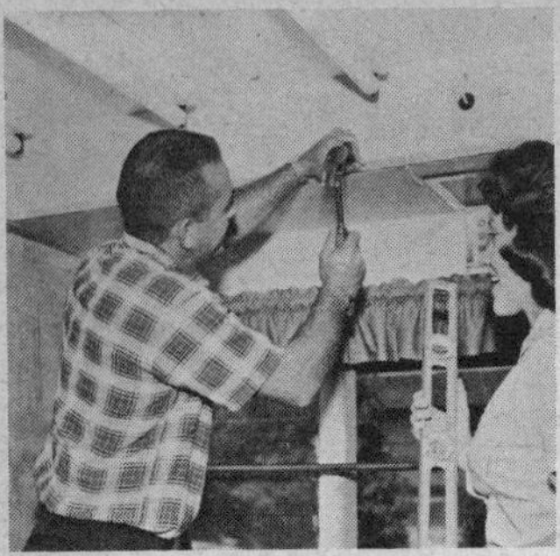
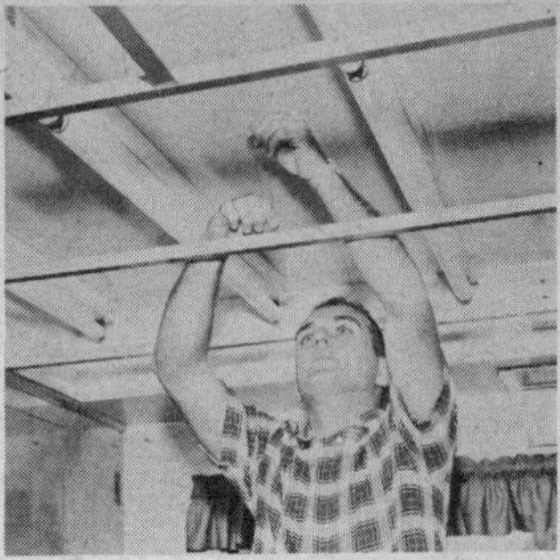
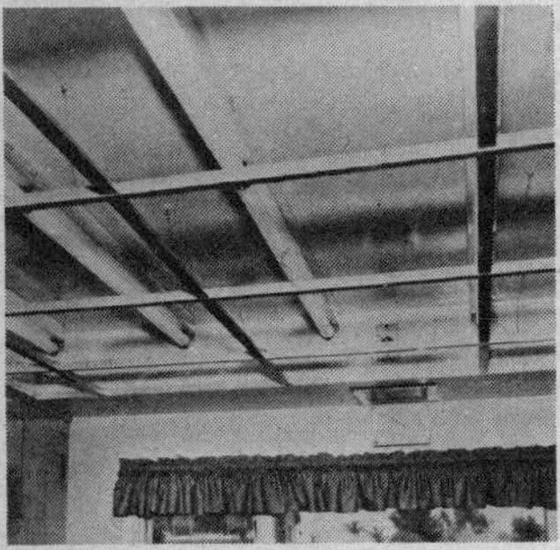
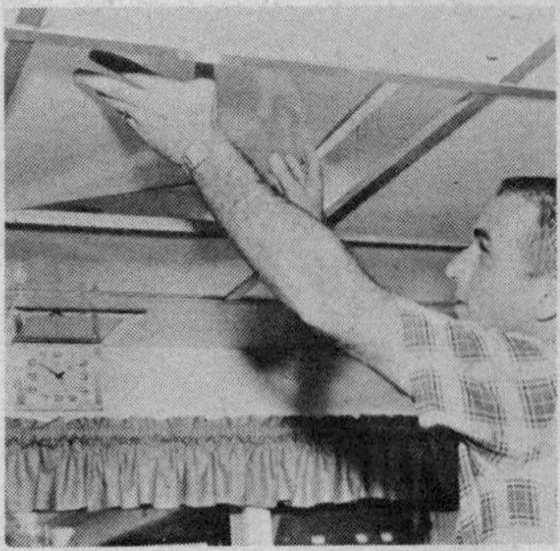
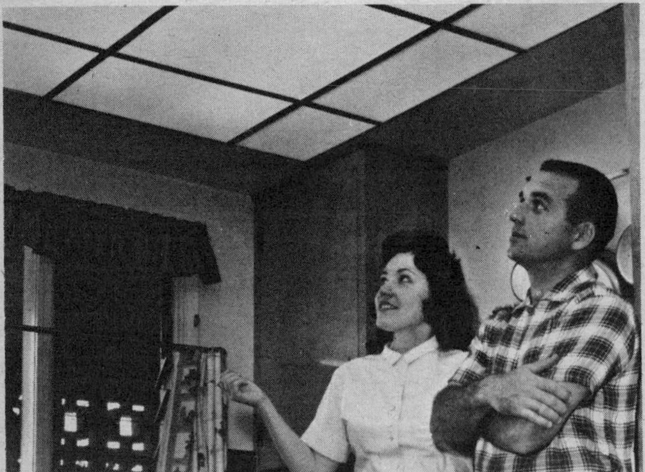

3 THE WALLS

- A Brick Wall—The Easy Way
- A Vinyl Wall
- Wipe-Clean Kitchen Paneling
- Put Your Walls To Work

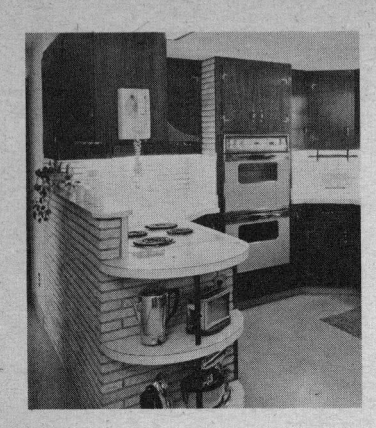

A BRICK WALL—
THE EASY WAY

For a rich, dramatic accent in the kitchen it's hard to beat a brick wall. But the special foundation required to support heavy masonry can be expensive.

An extremely realistic-appearing masonry substitute is now available in the form of individual bricklike facings that are only three eights of an inch thick, color-fast and lightweight.

The brick is available in various colors and textures. The modern kitchen shown at the top of this page combines the warmth of natural wood with white Roman brick for a most striking effect.

Remarkable authenticity is achieved by special manufacturing technique that gives each brick a rough or smooth finish faithful to its masonry counterpart. Colors are dead ringers for new or used brick and constant through each unit to preclude fading.

The bricks are thoroughly waterproof—as is the special mastic after drying—and can be washed with mild soap and water. They are also fire resistant, but are not recommended for firebox linings in a kitchen fireplace.

The brick substitutes are approximately the same length and height as regular bricks. Special pieces, pre-made in 90-degree-angle shapes, facilitate construction where around-the-corner covering is desired. Color choices include two shades of red (Early American and washed pink), pure white and dark brown.

The bricks can be installed over plywood, rock lath, cement and cement blocks or regular plastered walls. The surface to be covered must, of course, be structurally sound—free of loose wallpaper, dirt, grease, oil or scale. If you are in doubt, prime the surface with a coat of latex paint or affix plywood or rock lath over existing walls before applying the brick.

Installation is shown in photos above. Mastic is applied to the wall in a thin layer with a trowel or putty knife. Cover only an area that can be bricked in fifteen minutes. An alternate method is to coat the back of the brick with mastic, then position it on the wall. Photo at right above shows homeowner installing a vertical course at the ceiling line—brick is always installed from the top down.

The mastic sets up in about twenty minutes but you can make adjustments for nearly an hour. Be sure each course is level. To cut bricks, score the face about halfway through with a hacksaw, then snap off over countertop or other hard surface. Joints can be left rough or smoothed with a finger. Wash off the excess immediately.

A VINYL WALL

Not every do-it-yourselfer should attempt to install a vinyl wall covering material. But if you can honestly rate your handyman skills and experience a cut above the average, you should be able to include as part of your kitchen remodeling project a vinyl wall to which you can point with pride.

Vinyl wall covering material is flexible, yet tough. It will not tear easily when you handle it, but it is easy to cut with the proper tools. Only abnormal carelessness will cause it to tear or chip.

The Wall Corlon used in the installation shown on these pages is offered in three textures—knobby, striated, suede —two gauges and 20 colors. It has a water-resistant asbestos backing and comes in rolls 54 inches wide by approximately 90 feet long. Because its flexibility is affected by cold weather, it should be stored at room temperatures for at least 48 hours before installation.

The vinyl covering can be no smoother than the subwall over which it is installed. Old walls covered with wallpaper, wall coverings, calcimine or water-base paints should be stripped of the previous coverings and any hot spots in the plaster should be neutralized. Well-bonded oil or latex paints are suitable subsurfaces, but they should be scrubbed and then sanded lightly to provide proper bonding surface for adhesives. Textured walls of the stucco type should be first refinished with a smooth, well-bonded coat of white plaster.

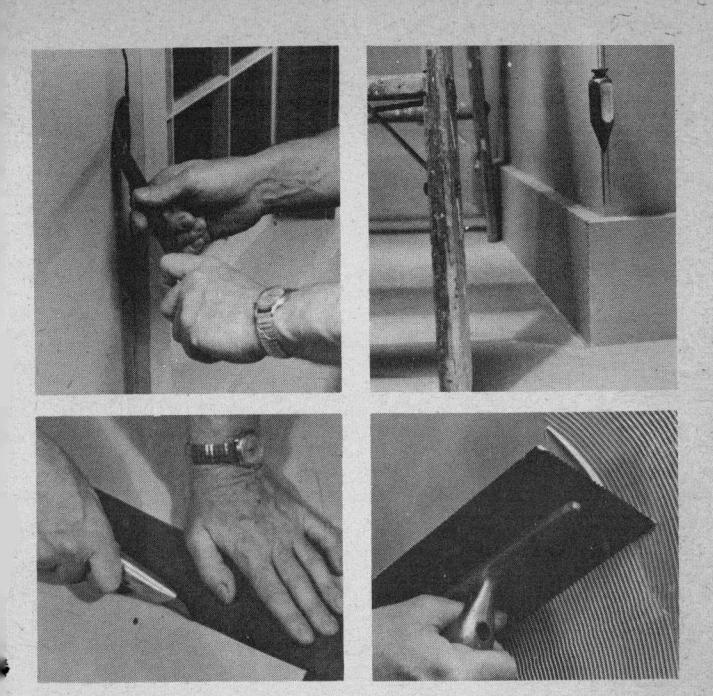

Start installation at a doorway—see photo at upper left. Moldings may be pulled away from the wall slightly so that vinyl can be slipped behind it.

Carefully lay out room before beginning actual installation. Check inside and outside corners for plumb, as shown in the next photo. Plan seams a minimum of four inches from corners. Also check level of ceiling line and, if you're planning wainscoting, strike a line the proper height, using both a level and a straight edge.

The material is cut to size on the floor or on a table, using a straight edge and a razor knife. Place scrap under cut to get a clean edge (photo left above). Cement may be applied to the wall with a fine-notched trowel (next photo).

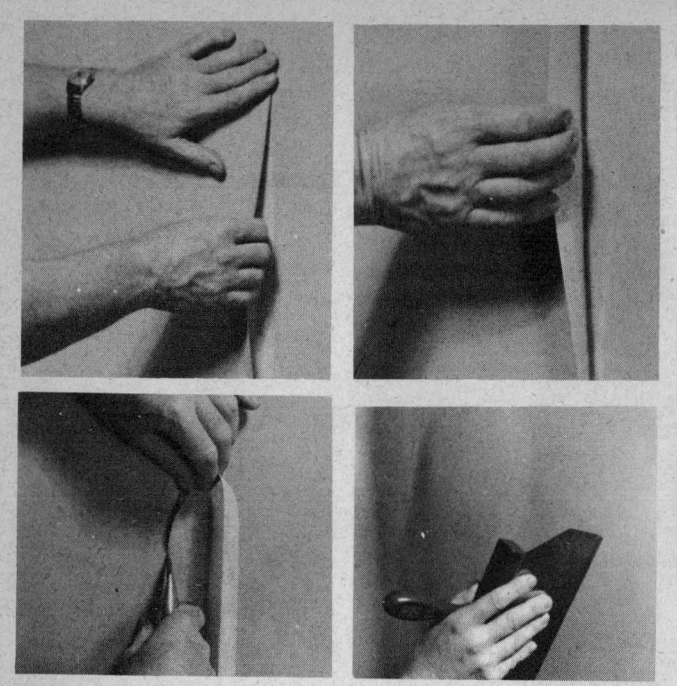

Roll strip of vinyl face in, butt to ceiling or wainscot line and unroll downward, smoothing it in place with a damp cloth.

There are two methods of seaming. If you are butting seams (top left photo), each succeeding piece is carefully placed against its neighbor. The alternate method calls for overlapping adjacent pieces 1 1/2 to 2 inches (next photo). Cutting, shown at left above, may be done free hand or with partner holding straight edge. Hold knife at an angle to hide the seam. Smooth out air pockets as shown at right, above, by pushing out with a broad knife. Use a sharp knife to prick material, if necessary, to let the air out.

Cement may also be applied directly to the material instead of the wall. Use either a brush or a lamb's wool roller. Fold the bottom part of the material up on itself for three-fourths of its length. Fold the top to meet. To apply, pull the short folded edge loose and butt against the ceiling or wainscot line. Unfold, smooth into place.

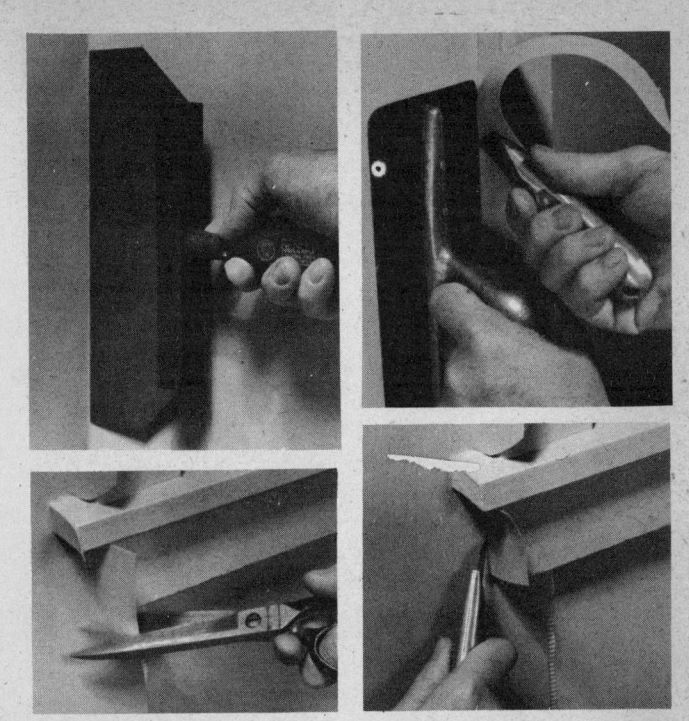

Material should extend around corners four or more inches. When forming inside corner, smooth material with damp cloth, use a broad knife to press into place, forming a sharp angle. See photo at top left.

Where corner is out of plumb, material will not align and excess must be trimmed when adjoining piece is installed. When trimming, cutting along ceiling line, door frame or baseboard, form material into a corner with a broad knife or trowel while removing the excess, as shown at top right.

Use shears to make cuts along the top and bottom of a window sill that juts out into the area you are covering with vinyl, as illustrated above. Then press material into place and cut away selvage with a razor knife.

WIPE-CLEAN WALL PANELING

The Early American kitchen shown above illustrates the effective use of several kinds of paneling in kitchen wall treatment. A woodgrain accent wall serves as the decorative focal point.

The "wood" is actually plastic-coated hardboard planks in an authentic woodgrain pattern. These are installed over horizontal furring strips nailed to the wall studs. Tongue-and-groove edges on the 16-inch wide planks simplify fitting. Concealed metal clips, which assure proper spacing, are nailed to the strips. Wallboard adhesive secures the planking to the backing.

The patterned material on the wall over the range and counter is also a plastic-finished hardboard panel. These are available in attractive mural scenes as well as various

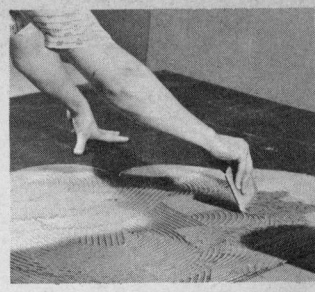

Installation of wood-grain planks over furring strips is shown in photo above. Adhesive is used to secure planks. Photo at top left shows application of mastic to wall panel. Positioning of scenic mural panel is shown at right. Several designs are available in addition to murals.

designs. The panels are applied directly over old walls (assuming that the walls are in good shape and not crumbling or pulling away from the studs) or any solid backing such as gypsum wallboard, plywood or hardboard.

Measure and trim panels. The adhesive is applied with a toothed spreader to assure an even, strong bond. Apply adhesive also to the wall.

The panel is then positioned on the wall. At the counter top it fits into a molding, which has been caulked to provide a watertight installation.

The plastic-finished planks and paneling are ideal for a kitchen installation, as they can be damp-wiped clean and never need refinishing. They are also highly resistant to moisture and heat.

PUT YOUR WALLS TO WORK

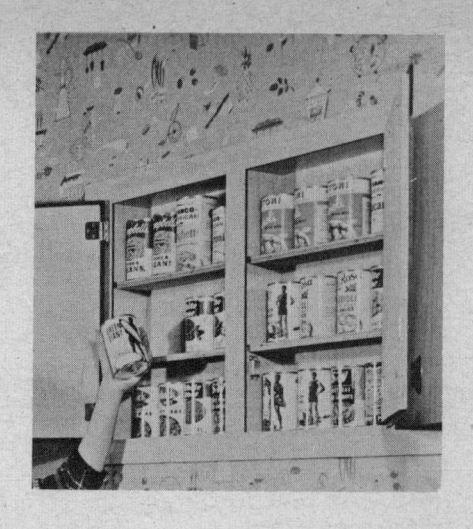

If your kitchen is that one in a million with adequate storage space for everything, read no further. For the rest of you, here's a way you can utilize that otherwise wasted space *within* a stud wall. It's just about perfect for storing canned goods and glass jars, freeing the regular wall cabinets for storage of bulkier items. No matter what material you use—or have already used—for finished wall surfaces, you'll be wise to consider putting this inner space to work.

The cabinets shown above were purposely built high on the wall so that the doors would clear the heads of persons seated at the kitchen table below them. If you desire to have lower cabinets in your kitchen, you can use the alternate construction suggested on the following pages and install sliding doors.

Basic construction of a single unit, showing standard dimensions and suggested materials, is shown in the diagram on the facing page. The parts are numbered in the order of installation.

The dimensions given apply only when wall studs are placed exactly 16" apart, measured from center to center, are full one and five eighths by three and five eighths inches in actual dimension and the wall ½" thick. Deviations, such as studs dressed undersize or inaccurately spaced, or wall thickness greater than ½", can be compensated for by cutting individual parts to fit as cabinets are assembled. Differences in dimensions will be so slight that all required material for a four-unit series of cabinets can be cut from one 4'x8' Marlite panel.

Construction is shown in the following photos and diagrams. Before cutting any wall openings, check the wall behind, in the basement and on the floor above to make sure that there are no plumbing or electrical conduits that will get in the way. Locate a wall stud and mark on the wall the area to be cut out. Use a level to mark the bottom and top of each opening. Drill holes at the corners of the marked-out area, then insert a keyhole of saber saw at these points and start cutting.

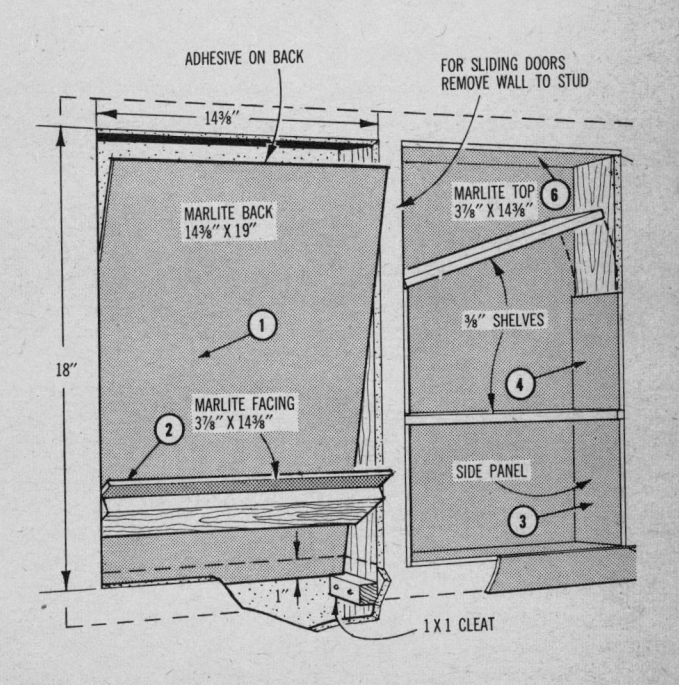

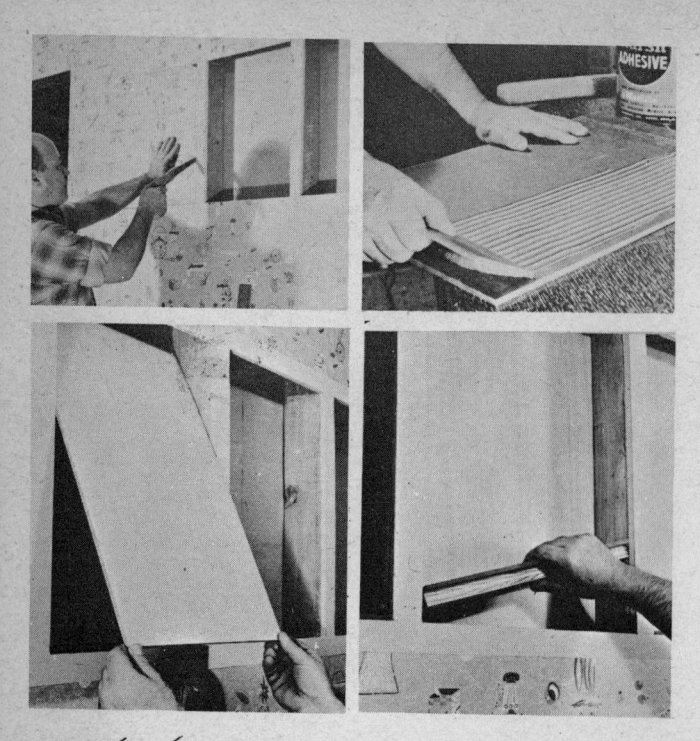

See photos above. Wall stud guides the blade in top left illustration. Use a notched spreader to apply adhesive to back panel after cleats are in place (top right). Positioning of cleats is shown in the earlier diagram. Lower left photo shows back panel being inserted—press solidly against wall and rest on cleats. Next is shown the placement of the bottom shelf panel, glued to plywood.

The 1"x1" bottom shelf cleats shown in the construction diagram are secured firmly in place, using glue and 6d finishing nails. When applying waterproof adhesive to the Marlite panels, allow a clear margin of 1 ½" around the edges so the adhesive will have a chance to spread when the panels are pressed in place. The plastic-finished hardboard can be cut with a circular saw, jigsaw or a fine-toothed hand saw. If a power jig is used, one that cuts on the upstroke, cut the Marlite with the finished side down.

The photos at the top of the page illustrate the next to last phases of construction. Pairs of side panels are cemented against studs to support shelves of paneling and plywood (top left).

After all the shelves are in place, attach facing trim. Top and bottom trim shown in photo at right is two inches wide. Side trim is three and three quarters inches.

Detailed diagrams for the construction of either hinged or sliding doors are shown on the following page.

Cut backs for the hinged doors from a three-foot square of three-eighths-inch plywood. Bond the Marlite facings to the plywood so that facing projects equally on all sides. This will form a three-eights-inch lip for overlapping the cabinet openings. Stack the doors together on a flat surface and weight the stack until glue has set. Three-eighths-inch offset hinges are used.

If you prefer sliding doors for your cabinet, remove the strips of wall-covering material from alternate studs so that each pair of sliding doors will cover two cabinets. Use aluminum ½-inch sliding door track as shown.

HINGE DOOR DETAIL

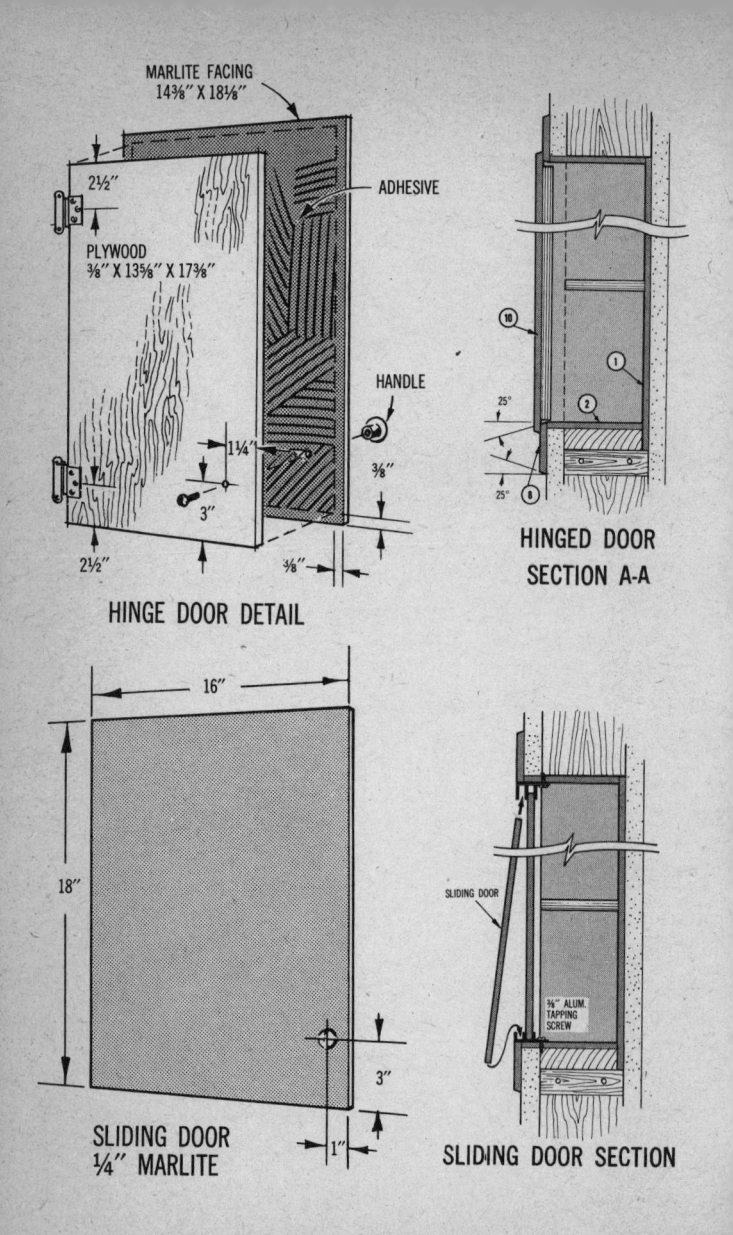

MARLITE FACING 14⅜" X 18⅛"
ADHESIVE
PLYWOOD ⅜" X 13⅝" X 17⅜"
HANDLE
2½"
1¼"
3"
2½"
⅜"
⅛"

HINGED DOOR SECTION A-A

① ② ⑩ ⑤
25°
25°

SLIDING DOOR
¼" MARLITE

16"
18"
3"
1"

SLIDING DOOR SECTION

SLIDING DOOR
⅜" ALUM. TAPPING SCREW

4 THE FLOOR
- **Tiling the Kitchen Floor**
- **The Kitchen Carpet**

TILING THE KITCHEN FLOOR

Resilient tile is the nearly unanimous choice of the handyman for covering the kitchen floor. Many types are available for the job, including rubber, cork, vinyl asphalt and vinyl-asbestos. Each has its advantages and less desirable qualities—you will find them listed at the end of this section describing the installation of a vinyl-asbestos flooring.

The do-it-yourselfer will find vinyl-asbestos tile a good choice for the kitchen floor.

Low in cost, easy to work with and simple to maintain, vinyl-asbestos tile is available in a wide variety of designs and colors and can be installed on any subfloor surface. Service gauge vinyl-asbestos tile is ideal for the amateur to install since it can be shaped with a pair of household scissors.

Whatever type floor tile you choose, the installation procedure will be just about the same as described on these pages—with the exception of cutting. The more brittle types must be heated before cutting, then shaped with a linoleum knife or special cutting machine.

Before you start your floor covering project, first assemble all the equipment you will need. Most of the tools are standard items from your home workshop—chalk and line, a four-inch paintbrush or notched trowel to spread the cement or mastic, a marking awl, a pair of scissors or other cutting tool, a ruler and pencil and a carpenter's square. For vinyl-asbestos tile, your dealer will supply you with a brush-on cement that is easily applied and requires no lining felt over the subfloor. A two-quart can covers an area of about 150 square feet.

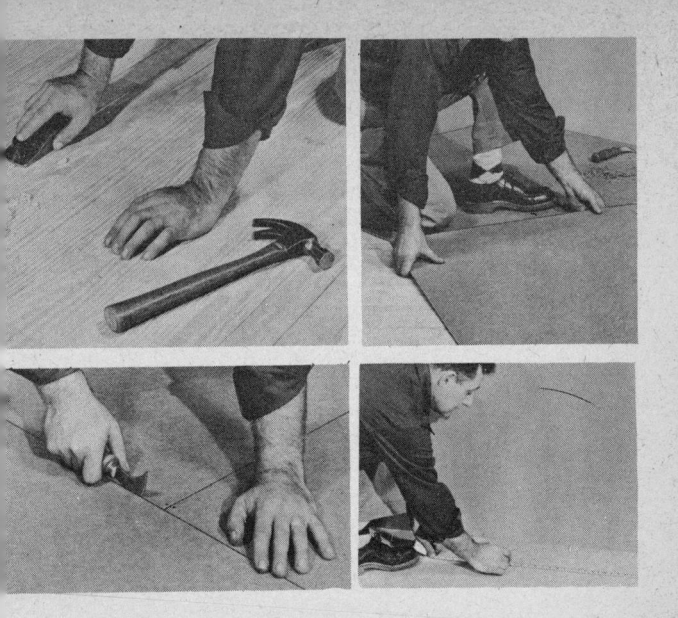

The appearance and length of service of your finished kitchen floor will depend a great deal on the condition of the subfloor. To prepare the subfloor, completely remove old floor coverings, wax, grease, dirt and paint. Plane down high spots and renail loose boards—see photo at top left. Holes or cracks in concrete floors of basementless homes should be repaired with crack filler, or damage to the tile may result.

Cracks in double wood floors should be filled with plastic wood. Where the floor is in extremely poor condition or there is only a single wood subfloor, cover the old floor with ¼-inch plywood or hardboard underlayment (top right photo). The underlayment should be installed with staggered joints about 1/32-inch wide to allow for expansion as illustrated at left, above. Fasten the underlay-

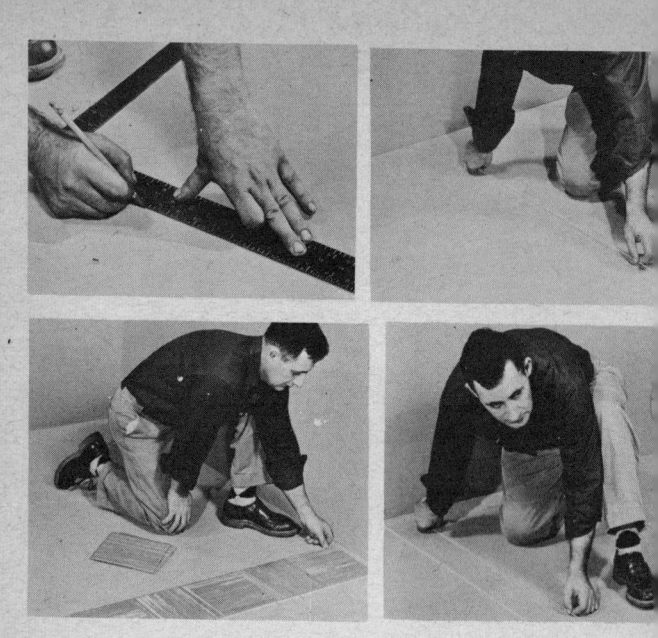

ment with coated or grooved nails spaced every four
inches along the edges and across the entire face of the
board. Make sure nails are driven flush with the surface so
that they will not show through the tile later on.

When you are satisfied with the condition of the subfloor, measure to find the center of each of the two end
walls of the room as shown in the last photo on the preceding page. Snap a chalk line down the middle of the
floor connecting these two points. Measure to locate the
center of this line. With a carpenter's square or the edge of
a tile, draw a perpendicular line on the floor (top left
photo). Along this line, strike another chalk line extending
to both side walls as at top right.

In one quarter of the room, along the chalk lines, lay
one test row of uncemented tiles (above, left) from the
center point to the side wall and one row to the end wall.
Measure the distance between the wall and the last tile

60

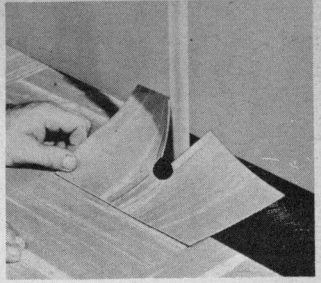

If the distance is less than two inches or more than eight inches, move the center line parallel to that wall 4 ½ inches closer to the wall (last photo on preceding page). This will assure the most economical usage of tiles and save the cutting of very narrow border tiles.

Spread a coat of cement over one quarter of the room, working from the chalk lines toward the walls. See photo at top left. Work into the corner and leave yourself a two-foot passageway along one way so you can back out. Allow the cement to dry about 30 minutes. It should feel tacky, but should not stick to your finger.

Starting at the intersection of the chalk lines, place the tiles in the cement, making sure that the first tiles are flush with the chalk lines and butted tightly against adjoining tiles. Do not slide tiles into place.

* This and subsequent steps for installation shown on last page of the article.

Fit the border tiles last. Place a loose tile exactly over the last full tile in the row. Then take another tile and place it on top of the first tile. Butt the top tile against the wall and use a pencil to mark the bottom tile along the edge of the top tile. Cut along this line and fit the cut portion of the tile into place.

To fit around pipes and other obstructions in the room, first make a paper pattern the same size as a 9x9 tile. Then fit it into the space as shown at right, page XX. Trace the outline of the pattern onto a tile and cut the tile to fit.

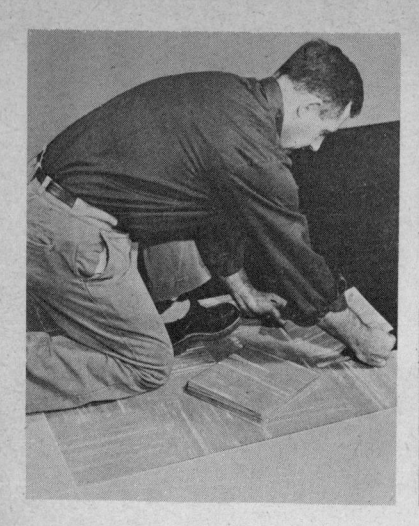

TILE TYPES (Lowest in cost listed first)	SPECIAL CHARACTERISTICS
Asphalt	Durable but brittle; may be harmed by oil, grease, solvents.
Grease-resistant asphalt	More durable and more flexible than asphalt and resistant to staining from grease, oil, solvents.
Linoleum	Somewhat porous and brittle.
Vinyl-asbestos	Has insulation value, fire resistance, hard surface.
Rubber	Brilliantly colored, very smooth finish. Slippery when wet; may be damaged by oil, grease, solvents.
Vinyl	Excellent wearing qualities; durable and flexible. Resists harsh cleaners.
Cork	Available in various shades of warm brown. Has good insulative and sound absorption value but stains easily.

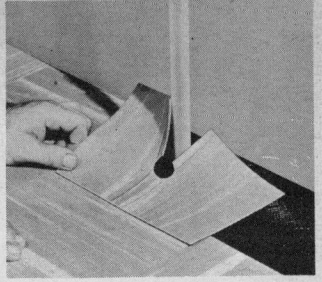

f the distance is less than two inches or more than eight
inches, move the center line parallel to that wall 4 ½ inches
closer to the wall (last photo on preceding page). This will
assure the most economical usage of tiles and save the cutting of very narrow border tiles.

Spread a coat of cement over one quarter of the room,
working from the chalk lines toward the walls. See photo
at top left. Work into the corner and leave yourself a two-foot passageway along one way so you can back out. Allow the cement to dry about 30 minutes. It should feel
tacky, but should not stick to your finger.

Starting at the intersection of the chalk lines, place the
tiles in the cement, making sure that the first tiles are flush
with the chalk lines and butted tightly against adjoining
tiles. Do not slide tiles into place.

* This and subsequent steps for installation shown on last
page of the article.

Fit the border tiles last. Place a loose tile exactly over
the last full tile in the row. Then take another tile and
place it on top of the first tile. Butt the top tile against the
wall and use a pencil to mark the bottom tile along the
edge of the top tile. Cut along this line and fit the cut portion of the tile into place.

To fit around pipes and other obstructions in the room,
first make a paper pattern the same size as a 9x9 tile. Then
fit it into the space as shown at right, page XX. Trace the
outline of the pattern onto a tile and cut the tile to fit.

TILE TYPES (Lowest in cost listed first)	SPECIAL CHARACTERISTICS
Asphalt	Durable but brittle; may be harmed by oil, grease, solvents.
Grease-resistant asphalt	More durable and more flexible than asphalt and resistant to staining from grease, oil, solvents.
Linoleum	Somewhat porous and brittle.
Vinyl-asbestos	Has insulation value, fire resistance, hard surface.
Rubber	Brilliantly colored, very smooth finish. Slippery when wet; may be damaged by oil, grease, solvents.
Vinyl	Excellent wearing qualities; durable and flexible. Resists harsh cleaners.
Cork	Available in various shades of warm brown. Has good insulative and sound absorption value but stains easily.

As each quarter of the room is finished, roll the tile with a linoleum roller. One can be borrowed or rented from your flooring dealer. Then follow the same process outlined above for each of the other quarters of the kitchen floor.

THE KITCHEN CARPET

A relative newcomer to the kitchen, carpeting is fast gaining favor as new spill-proof types are introduced.

A few years back, you would never have thought of covering your kitchen floor with carpeting. Now, thanks to the modern fibers used in the manufacture of many types of carpets, it is not only possible but a very practical choice in your kitchen remodeling project. Consider the advantages offered by a "soft" floor. For one thing, a carpeted kitchen is quieter, no small benefit in this noisiest room in the home. Too, carpeting offers warmth, comfort underfoot, and slip-proof qualities. And a piece of valuable crystal or china dropped on carpeting has a better chance of survival than if dropped on a harder floor surface.

With modern carpeting designed especially for kitchen use, you don't have to worry about stains and spots from spillage of such foods as eggs, ketchup, mustard and coffee—they can be sponged up in seconds. The outdoor-indoor carpet shown above is made of polypropylene olef[in] fiber which will not absorb moisture, thus reducing t[he] danger of permanent spotting. It is colorfast, non-shrink[-]ing, non-rotting and non-mildewing.

Available in a wide choice of colors, the carpeting come[s] in three-, six-, nine- and twelve-foot widths. It is easily in[-]stalled by the handyman. Waterproof cement can be use[d] for a permanent installation. If easy removal is desired, i[t] can be fastened in place with double-faced tape. Patter[n] designs can be made by carpet tiles obtainable in comple[-]mentary colors. Many striking and interesting effects ca[n] be achieved.

5 ELECTRICITY IN THE MODERN KITCHEN
- **Basics of Good Lighting**
- **Ventilation**
- **Custom-Built Range Hood**
- **Indoor Barbeque**

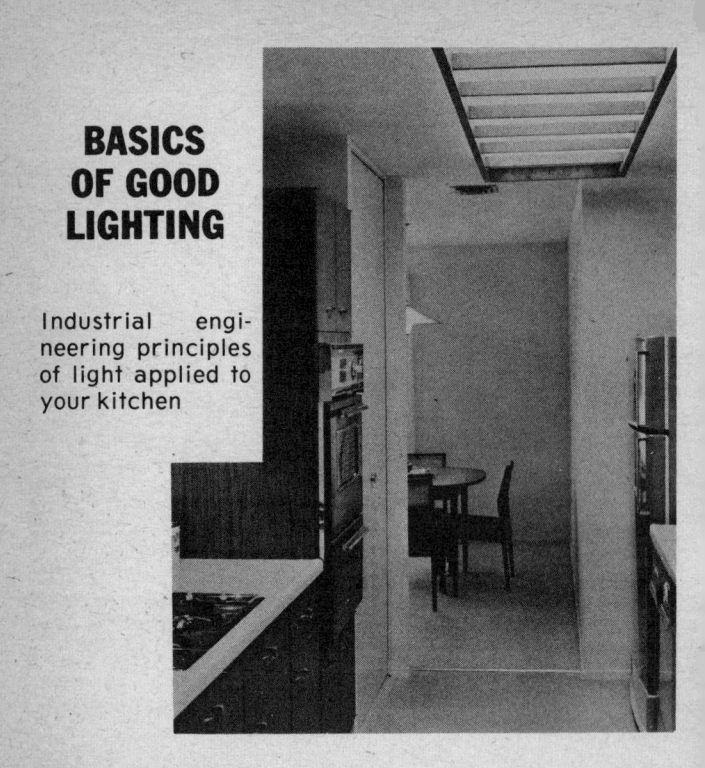

BASICS OF GOOD LIGHTING

Industrial engineering principles of light applied to your kitchen

Illustrated on this and the facing page are two examples of kitchen illumination serving opposite purposes. Above, a multipanel, "floating" lighted ceiling gives a small apartment kitchen an airy feeling of spaciousness. The photo on the next page shows a roomy kitchen with a wall-to-wall luminous ceiling providing overall illumination and special lighting—under-the-cabinet fixture over the range and bubble fixtures over the snack bar—dividing the room into specialized living-working areas.

Modern home planning and the many conveniences that are available actually bring today's kitchen much closer in function to the kitchen of the average early American home than it is to its more recent ancestor of forty or fifty years ago. Like its eighteenth and nineteenth century predecessor, the modern kitchen is more than a room for meal preparation, serving and cleaning up. It is a living center, an integral part of all the home activities and planning, but one which still retains its basic function as a work center. And today, work is subject to scrutiny under scientific principles that seek maximum efficiency and optimum working conditions.

Earlier we outlined some basic principles of planning a kitchen that is of equal importance to its dual role as a work and living area—adequate electrical provision, with particular emphasis on lighting and convenience.

Industrial engineers have long insisted that proper lighting is essential for any work area. To apply the scientific approach to kitchen lighting, let us set down the basic elements involved in what might be termed proper "light conditioning." These include the general light level, the specific light level (the light needed in a given area for a given task), the absence of glare, and brightness control (a well-lighted work area in an otherwise unlighted room is just as bad as a source of glare somewhere in your view).

You need light everywhere in the kitchen. It should be of sufficient intensity that you can easily read the small print on food packages. It should be evenly distributed so that you can see into cabinet corners, and so that you do not have to work in your own shadow. It should help to make the room cheerful and a pleasant place to work. In some kitchens, it may be possible to satisfy all these requirements by using carefully placed ceiling fixtures that do the job with virtually no additional local lighting fixtures. In most cases, however, general room lighting will be supplemented by specific lighting of particular work areas.

To provide general illumination, you could hardly do better than install a luminous ceiling, as described earlier in this book. The light given off is bright, well diffused and glareless. Ideally, the luminous ceiling should be extended from wall to wall, but smaller panels, centrally located, will also be effective, if properly coordinated with the specific lighting arrangements in the room.

Adequate and well-placed ceiling fixtures—either shielded fluorescent units or modern, smartly styled incandescent fixtures—can also be utilized to provide satisfactory general room lighting. These may be recessed or suspended below the ceiling. Or they may be built into a valance or soffit, shielded to direct light upward against a light-colored ceiling for general room illumination and spot-reflected downward for specific lighting purposes.

Whatever system of general illumination you plan for your kitchen, make sure that it permits no dark, shadowy corners or shadows in other areas.

The two kitchens illustrated above show contrasting methods of kitchen lighting. At right a ceiling dome light is used for overall room illumination. At left an eight-foot long, illuminated ceiling beam provides the principal source of light, but is supplemented by under-cabinet local lighting and two louvered down-lights over the cooking surface.

Proper specific light levels in such areas as food preparation counters, the range, the sink, and desks or telephone tables can be achieved through the use of fluorescent fixtures placed under wall cabinets over the particular area, or by directed spotlights attached to wall or ceiling. Make sure that such lights are placed so that one's own shadow will not fall on the work.

Glare can make a kitchen a most comfortable place in which to work. Fixtures that provide diffused illumination make the path of light much greater than its point of origin, thus minimizing the glare.

The photo above shows an example of soffit lighting, using decorative plastic panels to diffuse glare. The illustration on the facing page combines soffit lighting with fluorescent units over the counter and a hanging fixture over an island working area.

It is generally much easier to arrange lighting with fluorescent fixtures that provide lines of light rather than point sources, as do incandescent bulbs. Valances, cornices and coves are also useful in planning general lighting that shields the light source (and the glare) from the eyes. Where the entire ceiling (or large areas of it) is the source of light, there should be no brightness problem—no "hot spots" to distract and cause eye fatigue.

It is obvious that the kitchen consumes more electricity

than any other room in the home—the essentials of modern-day living demand it. Adequate wiring in the kitchen is an absolute necessity. Each major appliance should operate on its own individual electrical circuit, of course. But provision should also be made for other immediate and potential uses. Electric toasters, coffee makers, cookers, blenders, mixers, knife sharpeners, knives, juicers—all must be considered when planning an electrical layout for your kitchen.

Conventional duplex outlets should be spaced not more than four feet apart behind all counters and other work areas. Surface raceways and continuous outlet strips on individual circuits can be installed so that you can plug in your small appliances anywhere along the work counter. Always be sure to use grounded outlets near the sink.

These suggestions should serve as your guide to planning your electrically up-to-date kitchen. Your local utility company will be familiar with codes and ordinances that must be complied with.

A KITCHEN VENTILATION SYSTEM

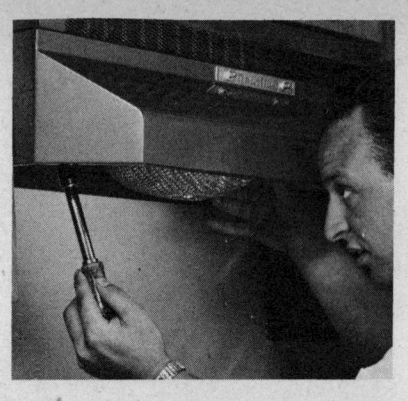

A kitchen ventilating system is no luxury—you need it to keep cooking smoke, grease and moisture from damaging your home. Over 200 pounds of smoke, moisture and greasy vapors are given off each year during the cooking process in the average American home. In baking a typical 12-pound ham, for one instance, 3 pounds of its original weight will be distributed in the form of such by-products as greasy vapors and carbon deposits. If not removed, these deposits will settle on the walls and furnishings throughout the house. The moisture given off in the cooking process creates a vapor pressure than can penetrate the walls and roof of the home. In cold weather this flow of moisture condenses within the walls in the form of frost. When the frost thaws out, the resulting moisture causes deterioration of insulation and siding which in many cases is followed by paint blistering.

With approximately 70 per cent of the heated food preparation in the average home done on the surface unit, it is obvious that some means must be employed to control moisture and greasy vapors before they are able to inflict serious damage. An exhaust system, with a fan located as closely as feasible to the surface cooking unit, will remove up to 98 per cent of these greasy vapors and moisture.

Several types of systems are available. A popular type of exhaust system is a range hood with a built-in fan. A good unit properly installed will draw off much of the grease, moisture and cooking odor before it has a chance to escape into the kitchen. The air will then be discharged out of doors (perhaps after passing through a filter or series of filters to trap the grease).

A custom-built range hood is shown on the opposite page. Most homeowners undertaking a kitchen remodeling job will not bother with making their own range hoods. However, not all manufactured units are as generously shaped as this one, nor as functional as far as removing odors is concerned.

Photo shows a rectangular vent leading to an exhaust system above the hood, but a small, efficient ventilating fan can also be located in the wall under the hood to exhaust odors.

The diagram shown for the lower part of the hood is self-explanatory. Dimensions and procedure are shown. Recommended material is stainless steel, but the design can also be adapted to copper, in case you feel that the latter is more suited to a provincial or country-style kitchen.

The pattern for the one-piece main section of the hood can be laid out on kraft paper first and then transferred to the sheet metal.

If you feel that a job like this is for a sheet-metal man rather than for the home workshop, you can have a local shop cut it out and assemble it for you.

Range hood-fan-light units may also be purchased ready for home installation and to fit modern decor.

Other types of exhaust units are built into the wall, directly over the range, or into the ceiling. These, too, discharge objectionable wastes out of doors, though generally not as effective as a hood-type unit. But they are satisfactory in most cases.

Venting the fan to the outside is an important factor in

PATTERN FOR LOWER HOOD SECTION

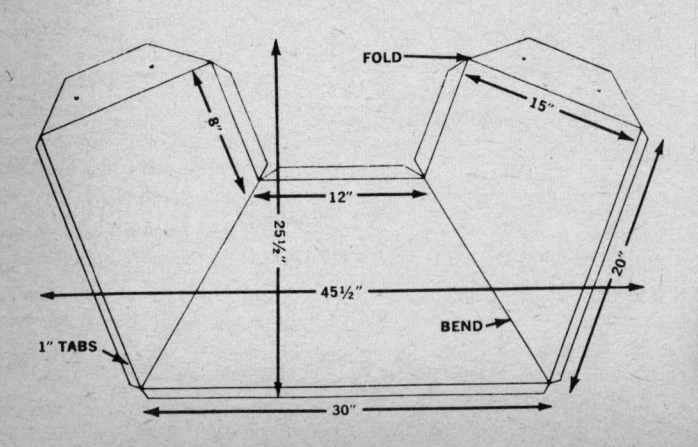

FOLD

8"

15"

12"

25½"

45½"

20"

1" TABS

BEND

30"

determining fan location. The best and simplest way, if kitchen layout allows it, is to have the fan vent directly through the wall to the outside. If ductwork is necessary, as in a ceiling installation or where the fan is located on an inside wall, it should be as short and as straight as possible. Each 90-degree turn cuts down air flow by almost a third, and also acts as a trap for grease that is being moved through the duct.

Another consideration in choosing and locating a fan is the normal air flow through the room. If air coming into a kitchen will be drawn right into the fan, it will divert the smoke and cooking odors throughout the kitchen. In the case of a hood suspended over an island or peninsula range, the installation is subject to cross drafts and the fan size should be increased substantially.

A hood over a peninsula-mounted range is illustrated above, left. The photo at right shows a ductless, disappearing hood fitted over a wall oven—canopy, shown open here, closes flush with the surface when oven is not in use.

Where it is not feasible to install a fan vented to the outside, a ductless type may be used. These also utilize an electric fan. This draws the vapors and grease from the cooking surface through a series of filters, then recirculates the air toward the ceiling. The filters are highly effective in removal of grease, and certain types of good quality are also effective in removal of smoke and cooking odors. They are less effective in control of cooking heat, though they do dissipate it by discharging it back into the room toward the ceiling.

A simple installation of a ductless range hood unit is shown in the photo at the beginning of this article. This particular unit is held in place by four wood screws.

Proper use of electricity in the kitchen now enables you to say, regardless of season of the year or the weather outside:

"LET'S HAVE A BARBEQUE!"

The popularity of charcoal cookery has become so great that it has inevitably moved indoors and shown above is a portable unit that can be used either indoors or out.

There's no reason for you to either wait for summer or else shiver in the cold and snow while tending to a sputtering fire and a sizzling steak that can be done only *one* way to bring out its delicious succulence. Now you can have that steak every day of the year—budget permitting. All you need to do is include a barbecue grille in your kitchen remodeling program.

Such a unit can be as elaborate or as simple as you wish. If, for example, your plans include a masonry fireplace wall, perhaps separating the kitchen from the living room, you might build a second fireplace facing into the kitchen, with an incorporated open-cooking area. More likely, though, you will be doing things on a more modest scale. In this case, you'll simply drop a prefabricated barbecue unit into an opening cut into a countertop, install a large-sized hood-fan over it—and let those steaks sizzle away.

These barbecue units are available with regular charcoal firing, as well as with gas burners or electric cooking elements. In the gas models, radiant ceramic "coals" above the burner hold and evenly distribute the cooking heat; the electric models usually have a layer of ceramic below the element to distribute the heat.

Most of the units are encased in insulated shells and can be safely installed in wood or metal kitchen cabinetry, as well as built into brick, stone or concrete block, indoors or out. Some units are designed for masonry only, with open sides, back and bottom, so make sure you buy the right type for your purposes. Most units also offer a motorized rotisserie as an extra.

To adequately exhaust cooking aromas and charcoal smoke from indoor areas, a hood and fan with a capacity rated at least 600 cubic feet per minute (CFM) are recommended. Manufacturers' ratings will be noted on the fan nameplate. The hood should extend at least one inch beyond each edge of the barbecue unit. In the case of an island or peninsula unit where cross drafts are a factor, it should extend at least 3 inches beyond each edge. The bottom of the hood should be from 16 to 24 inches above the barbecue, with 30 inches the absolute maximum.

If your kitchen is on a level with a backyard patio or

wood deck, you can combine your indoor and outdoor barbecuing in one portable unit. These are available for charcoal, gas or electric fuels with special gas and electric fuel extension kits, or even with an LP gas tank. Just wheel the unit in or out, depending on the time of year and the weather. Make sure that here, too, you have an adequate exhaust system where you use the unit indoors.

Shown above is a rotisserie, available with most barbecue units. Perhaps the simplest indoor barbecue to install is a drop-in gas unit, completely encased, requiring only a cutout in a counter, cabinet space below and accessibility to your fuel line.

6 CABINETS

- Kitchen Cabinet Construction
- Assemble-it-Yourself Cabinets
- Kitchen Corner Cabinets
- Get Yourself Organized
- Let Lazy Susan Do The Work
- Special Storage Ideas

KITCHEN CABINET CONSTRUCTION

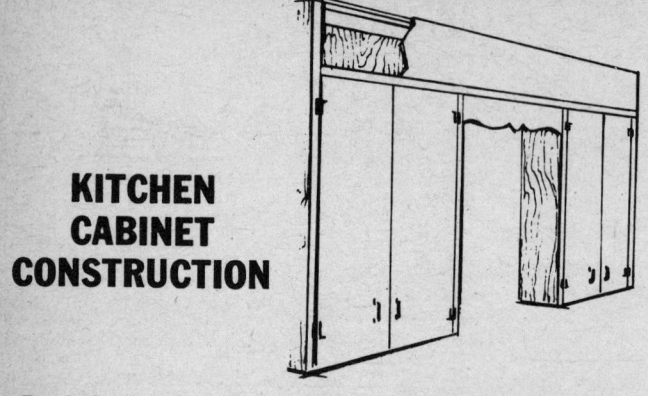

Buy? Or build your own? The decision is for you to make. The cabinets you choose for your kitchen are of utmost importance to its design and function. Adequate cabinet storage space is a major but necessary item.

Although it is possible for the handyman to build his own cabinets, using only hand tools, the task is one not to be undertaken lightly. A homeowner with a complete set of power tools is able to get the job done much faster and with better results.

Wall cabinets for the kitchen are generally manufactured in either 30" or 33" heights. Cabinets for use above the range or the refrigerator are usually less—from 12" to 15" in height. Widths will vary, of course, and this is where the advantage of custom-built cabinets shows up. No filler strips are required where cabinets are built to fit an exact space.

Similarly, wall cabinets can be constructed to ceiling height, making it unnecessary to box in the soffit area at the top. Soffit area detail of a customized wall cabinet is diagrammed above. Pine fascia board may be nailed over soffit area at the top or an illuminated panel may be installed. Or the space may be left accessible for storage. Soffit immediately above the sink has fascia with a scalloped edge.

Select knotty pine paneling is recommended, regardless of how the cabinets will be finished, even for the doors, which are battened on the backs and, in the illustration, hung with antique hinges.

Diagrammed above are some construction details of a wall cabinet. Figure at top left shows wall cleat nailed to the studs at the desired height to support the cabinet. An inner member of the cabinet rests on the cleat and is also nailed to the studs. The drawing at top center shows adjustable hardware shelf supports, which are optional but enable you to utilize space most effectively.

The bottom cleat shown at top right may also be fastened to the studs.

Basic cabinet construction in the home work shop is illustrated in the photos on the next pages. Simple framework for a cabinet intended for hardwood or other light facing and sliding doors requires only hand tools and the accompanying captions and text are self-explanatory. The framework members grooved to receive the quarter-inch sliding doors may be purchased.

The unit shown is intended for storage—suit the dimensions for your particular purpose and space.

Lumber consists of 1" x 2" pieces cut to length and the two grooved members that will receive the doors. These are purchased in sets—one member is more deeply grooved—and come in varying lengths. During construction remember to place the deeply grooved member on top.

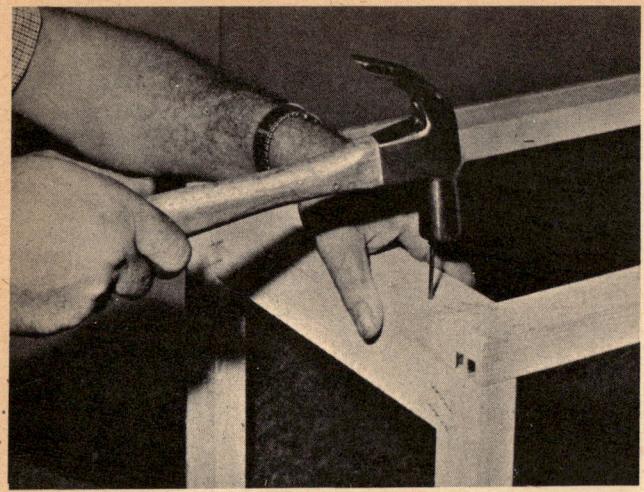

Assembly of the framework for a simple cabinet is shown above. Parts are joined by corrugated fasteners, then nailed. Snakelike glue line is applied (below) in preparation for panel. Method creates firm bond.

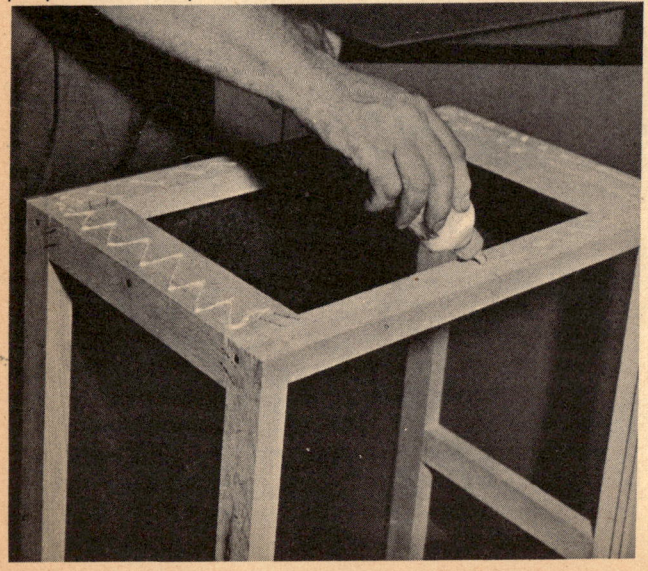

STORAGE UNIT

Hardboard triangle helps brace back of framework during construction, as in top left photo. View underneath (top right) shows lumber supports for shelves nailed to side panel. Hardboard shelves are simply dropped into place. Screws driven into countersunk holes hold back panel in place, left above. Inside view (right, above) reveals cross bracing and grooved framework for sliding doors.

ASSEMBLE-IT-YOURSELF CABINETS

Forward-looking manufacturers have made it possible for the tool-less homeowner to have his cake and eat it, too, by packaging cabinets in knocked-down form. You have your choice of wood or sheet steel units. Both kinds can be assembled easily, requiring neither special tools nor special skills. The photos show how it is done.

Hardwood cabinets are manufactured in standard sizes with filler strips available to fill odd spaces.

Illustrated on this and the following pages is the assembly of a ponderosa pine cabinet. White polyvinyl glue and finishing nails are used to secure all structural joints. Glue lines are run in the grooves of the prefabricated cabinet units, as shown in the top photo on the facing page. Pieces then are tapped together with a mallet or a hammer and a wood block, as above.

The finishing nails lock all joints for proper glue adhesion and additional strength. See lower left photo on facing page. Drive nails in carefully and set slightly below surface with nail set.

Right hand photo shows installation of sliding shelf in a base cabinet. Cleats are screwed to frame to prevent the shelf's tipping. A door stop will also be attached.

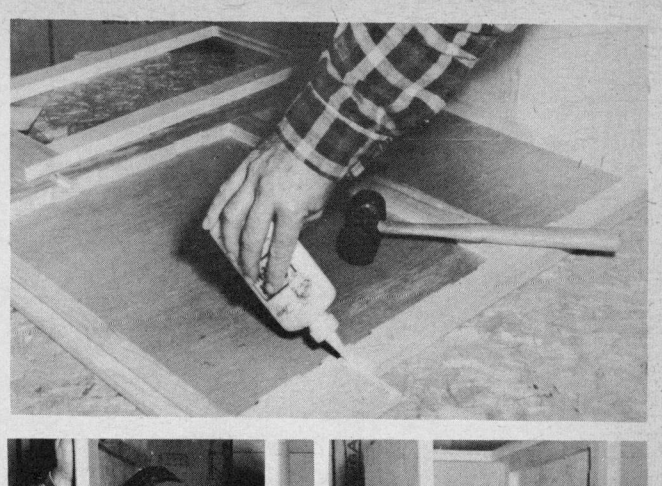

Cabinets, shelves, doors, and drawers are assembled and, if desired, prefinished; then the base cabinets are set in place on a kickboard base frame. Wall cabinets are mounted with the aid of a wooden strip nailed temporarily to the wall; the cabinets are then fastened permanently to wall studs.

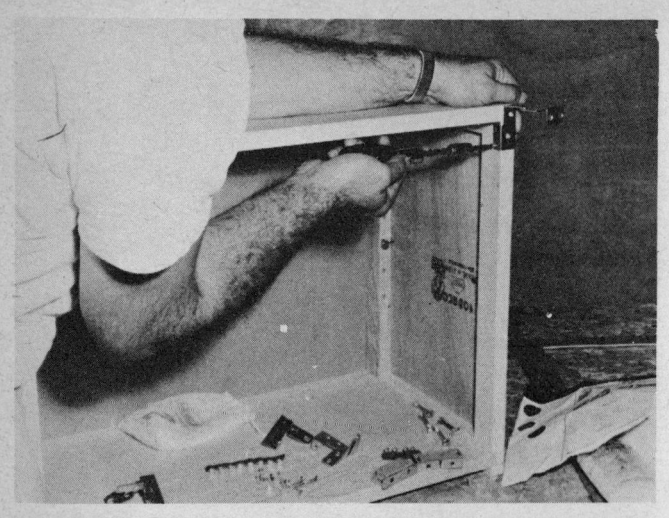

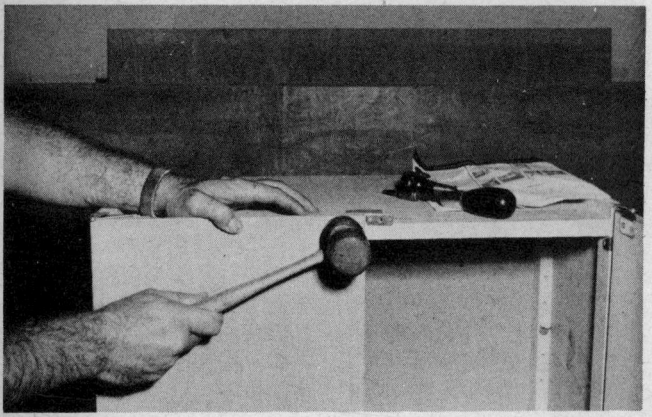

Details are shown on this and the facing page.

Upper photo shows hardware installation before cabinets are set in place. Concealed hinges supplied by the manufacturer will fit into prefabricated door cutouts. In the lower photo the door is tapped lightly to locate exactly the fastening for the magnetic catch.

Both wall and base cabinets are prefabricated in units. Build as many as will meet your space or storage requirements. Units are then pulled and locked together by drilling holes and inserting special bolts provided, as shown in photo above, left.

Base cabinets are then set on kickboard base frame.

To aid in mounting wall cabinets, a wood cleat is temporarily nailed to the wall along the bottom line—the cleat is shown in photo at right, above, under the cabinet and protruding slightly to the right. This helps to support the cabinet until it is located exactly as you want it and permanently screwed to the wall studs.

The metal cabinets, which can be assembled with a screwdriver, are available with wood veneer inserts for the door fronts, or plastic laminate may be substituted if desired. This allows you to change the decor of your kitchen with relative ease. Doors can be mounted to swing in either direction. Base cabinets are equipped with built-in leveling bolts to compensate for uneven flooring. The wall cabinets hang on special brackets.

The cabinets are available in a variety of sizes and colors

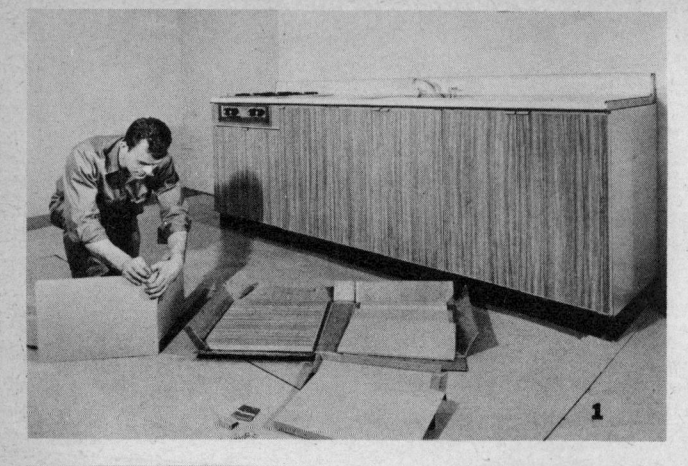

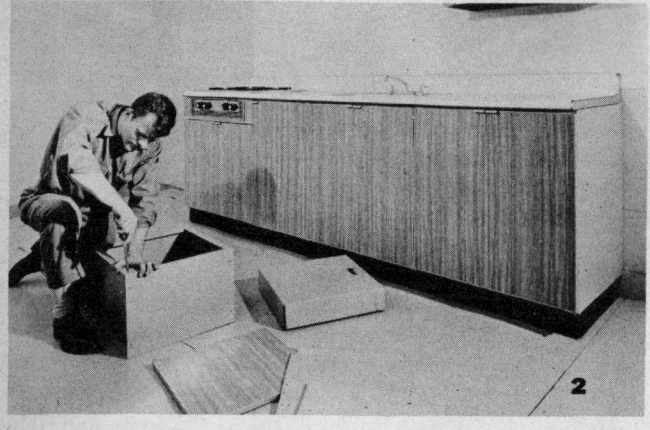

—even wood grain finish—to fit your decor. The simple steps of assembly and installation are shown in the numbered photographs above and on next page.

The cabinet pieces are fitted together (1), and fastened with Phillips head screws (2) that are provided with the package. The mounting of the doors—provision is made for them to be mounted to swing in either direction—is shown in photo 3.

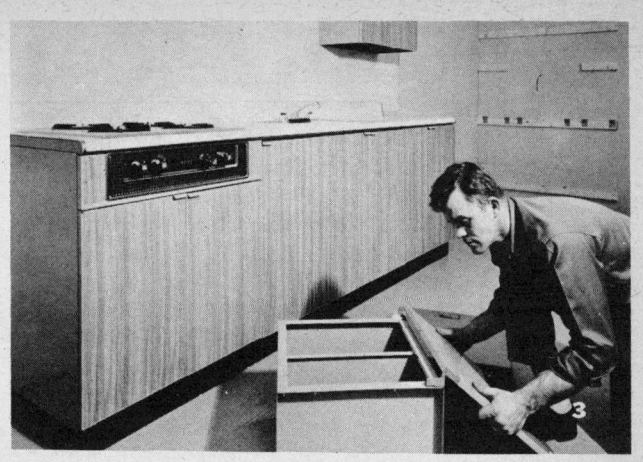

Leveling bolts for installation on uneven flooring come with individual units and are invisible under the base cabinet kickboards. The wall cabinets are hung on special mounting brackets that have been fastened to wall studs (4).

Metal cabinets are maintenance free and virtually indestructible. It is possible to order them custom-painted to suit your taste and individual preference.

Trade unused space for storage and counter area with these built-in

KITCHEN CORNER CABINETS

No one has ever counted the kitchens in which a wasted corner just stands there, doing nothing. If such a census were taken, it would be found that for every such kitchen there's a disgruntled housewife, giving said corner the evil eye. Mr. Edward Goldenberg, Jr., Valley Stream, N.Y., brightened that corner and pleased his wife by designing and building the handsome cabinets you see here.

This built-in adds counter surface and storage space to the kitchen, and uses its corner location to advantage. The shape of the lower cabinet allows free passage between the doorways on either side, and permits access to the work surface from all angles. Its two doors are positioned so that all parts of the deep storage shelves can be reached without strain. Up above, the top cabinet fits the corner neatly, and its triangular shape means you don't bump your head while working at the counter.

The unit is built of plywood and 1" lumber, and presents no construction difficulties. All dimensions and lumber sizes are shown in the sketch on the following page. Simple instructions are given below.

The first step is to nail all the shelf-supporting cleats through the wall surface to the studding. Also nail the cleat at the very top to the ceiling joists. Note that the ends of the cleats for the upper cabinet must be cut at an accurate 45-degree angle along the edges that meet the walls.

Nail the lower cabinet shelves to the cleats and build the cabinet framing around them. The facing for the cut-off corner is a length of 1x6 with its long edges beveled to a 45-degree angle. Fasten the shelf-supporting cleats to this piece before fitting it in place, then nail the shelves to these cleats from inside the cabinet. The counter top of ¾" plywood is nailed in place to complete the lower cabinet.

The doors are made of two layers of plywood—each door is a piece of ¾" plywood with a piece of ¼" plywood nailed over it to provide a ½" overlap around the edges. Use offset cabinet hinges to hang the doors, then add suitable handles and door catches.

Cover the counter top with laminated plastic and apply stainless steel or aluminum trim to the edges. The cabinets are trimmed with wood moldings where they meet the floor and ceiling. Before painting the unit, counterset all exposed nail heads, conceal with wood putty and sand smooth when dry. Choose your paint colors to match either the adjacent walls or the other cabinets in the kitchen, depending on your decor—or separation desired if the new cabinet serves both kitchen and dinette.

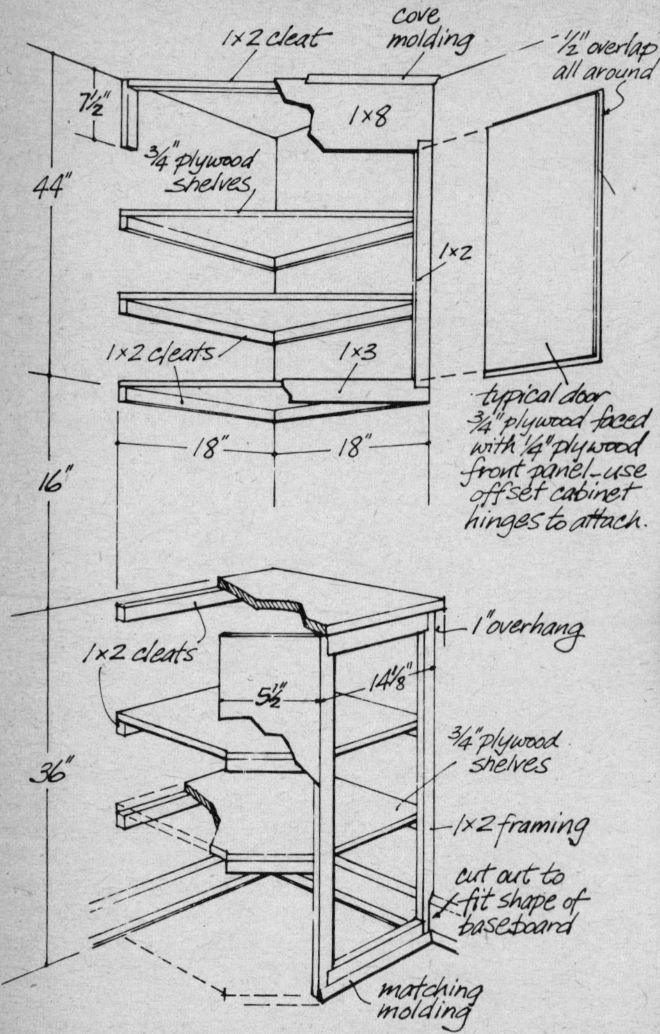
1×2 cleat
cove molding
1/2" overlap all around
7 1/2"
1×8
3/4" plywood shelves
44"
1×2
1×2 cleats
1×3
typical door 3/4" plywood faced with 1/4" plywood front panel-use offset cabinet hinges to attach.
18"
18"
16"
1" overhang
1×2 cleats
14 1/8"
5 1/2"
3/4" plywood shelves
36"
1×2 framing
cut out to fit shape of baseboard
matching molding

The final photo shows the finished cabinet at work. The reach-through feature of the twin doors makes the lower cabinet particularly useful for storage of "busy" items—everything is within easy reach, minimizing the need for constant and rigid organization of contents. The triangular shape of the upper shelves lends itself to similar functionalism.

The decorative effect when the cabinets are not in use has a sculptural quality in that it transforms space by adding a new dimension to it, both real and aesthetic.

GET YOURSELF ORGANIZED

Four novel ideas are incorporated in the compact kitchen organizer shown above.

It compacts several very attractive features. The sliding doors, for instance, are also small bulletin and blackboards. One is finished with blackboard paint, the other with a magnetic material or thin cork. The inside door must be used for the blackboard.

A spacious shelf above accommodates every cookbook your favorite chef has accumulated, while the four drawers can be used for filing favorite recipes, kitchen utensils, bills, and so on. The section at the lower left is shown covered with an optional fixed panel, to which a telephone is fastened. If your kitchen phone is not this type, the panel can be omitted and the interior space used for the phone instead.

Construction, as shown in the sketch, is rabbeted throughout, but butt joints may also be used if dimensions are adjusted. No back is necessary. The cabinet can be screwed to cleats nailed to studs so that the bottom of each shelf will rest on them.

Materials needed for construction are two pieces of 33

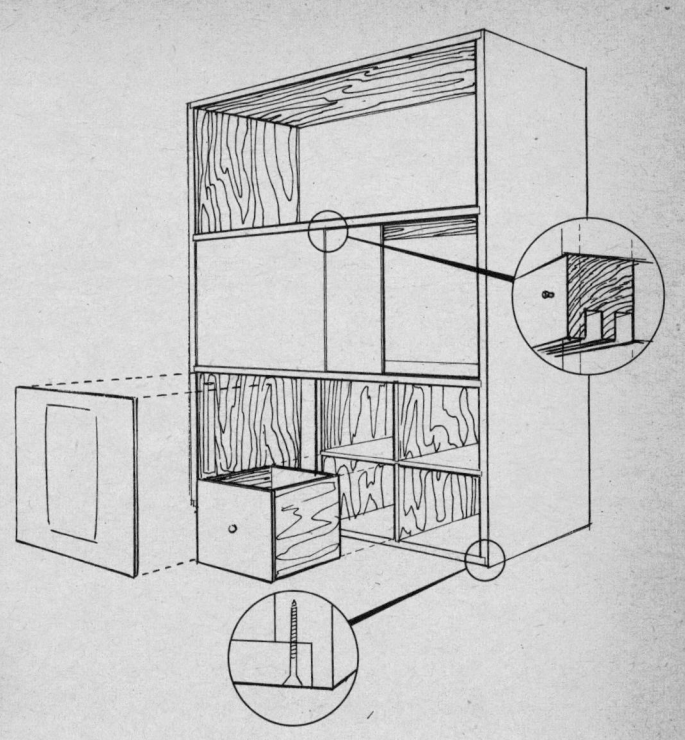

x 10 x ¾" lumber for sides and two 23 ½ x 10 x ¾" pieces for top and bottom. Two pieces, 23 ½ x 9 x ¾", make the two center shelves. Two pieces, 12 ½ x 10 ½ x 1/8", are needed for the hardboard doors. The vertical shelf dividers are made of two 10 ½ x 10 x ¾" pieces of lumber. The horizontal drawer separator consists of a single piece, 10 ¾ x 10 x ¾ inches. The 10-7/8 x 10 x ½" phone panel is optional. A 1 x ¾" sliding door track and two pieces, 1 x ¾", for cleats complete the main cabinet assembly. The drawers require four 5 x 4-5/8 x ½" fronts, eight 8 x 4-5/8 x ½" sides, four 4 ½ x 4-1/8 x ½" backs, and four 7 x 4 x ½" bottoms.

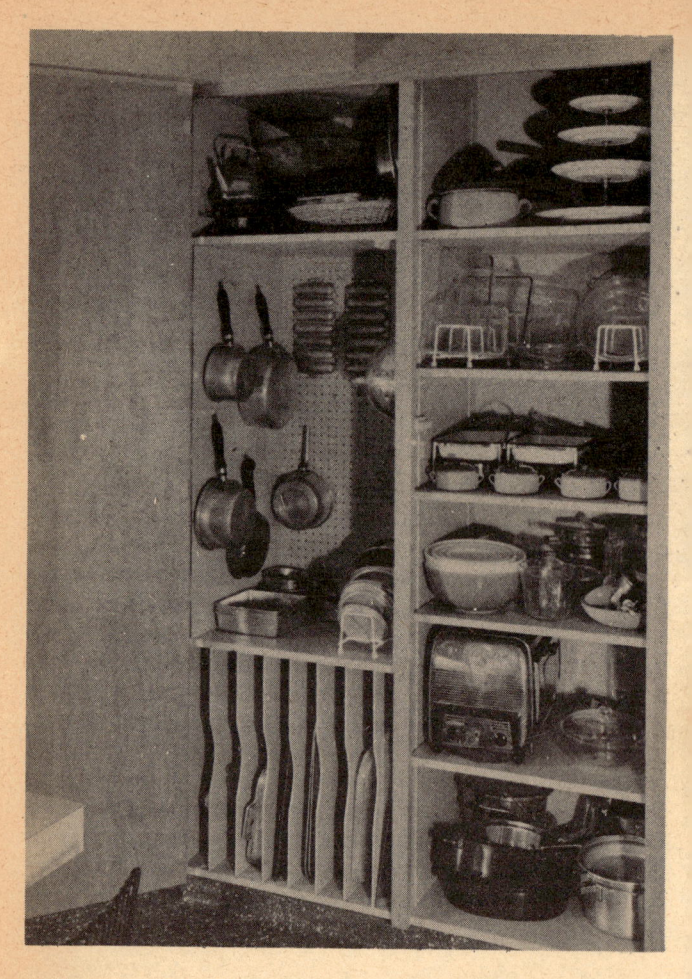

An organized kitchen is a spacious kitchen and what better way to organize than with a catch-all closet such as the one shown above?

The unit diagrammed is fully flexible to meet your particular storage needs. No inside dimensions are given —make them your individual family's life-size. If your kitchen is designed for indoor-outdoor cooking, the pegboard compartment can be designed to hold barbecue tools or equipment.

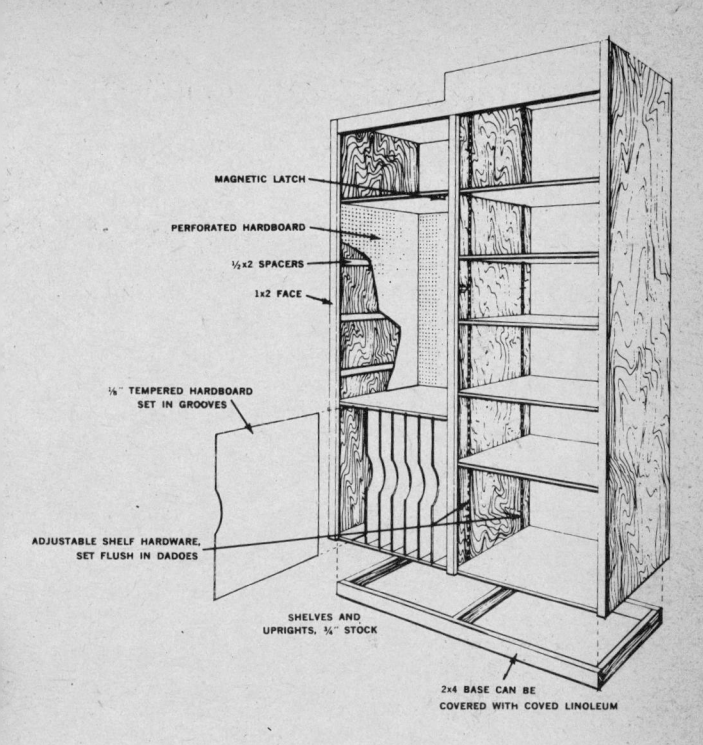

Floor-to-ceiling height is a necessity to take full advantage of what it has to offer, but width is optional. If available space doesn't permit duplication of the full unit, build half, suiting the interior to your personal needs.

Cut and assemble the component parts on a 2x4 base, which can be covered with coved linoleum later to match the floor. Doors are cut from ¾ inch plywood and hung on offset hinges to allow them to close flush. If your kitchen is wood-paneled, as this one is, use matching stock for the frame and cabinet doors.

LET LAZY SUSAN DO THE WORK

The junction of two busy counters, such as those shown above, where two banks of cabinets meet at right angles is often wasted but can be salvaged easily for added convenience. Assuming that the cabinet depth is identical in both arms of the angle, as is usually the case, the wasted space is a square, a shape that lends itself perfectly to the idea shown here. A special set of commercially available lazy-susan hardware, installed as diagrammed on the facing page, makes it possible. The number of shelves and their spacing is left to the individual. The shelves are screwed to the flanges; the vertical separators are edge-nailed. The doors are then nailed to the shelves or attached to them from the back with small angle brackets and screws. Fence the edges of the shelves with any flexible material to prevent stored items from falling off.

CAP STRIP

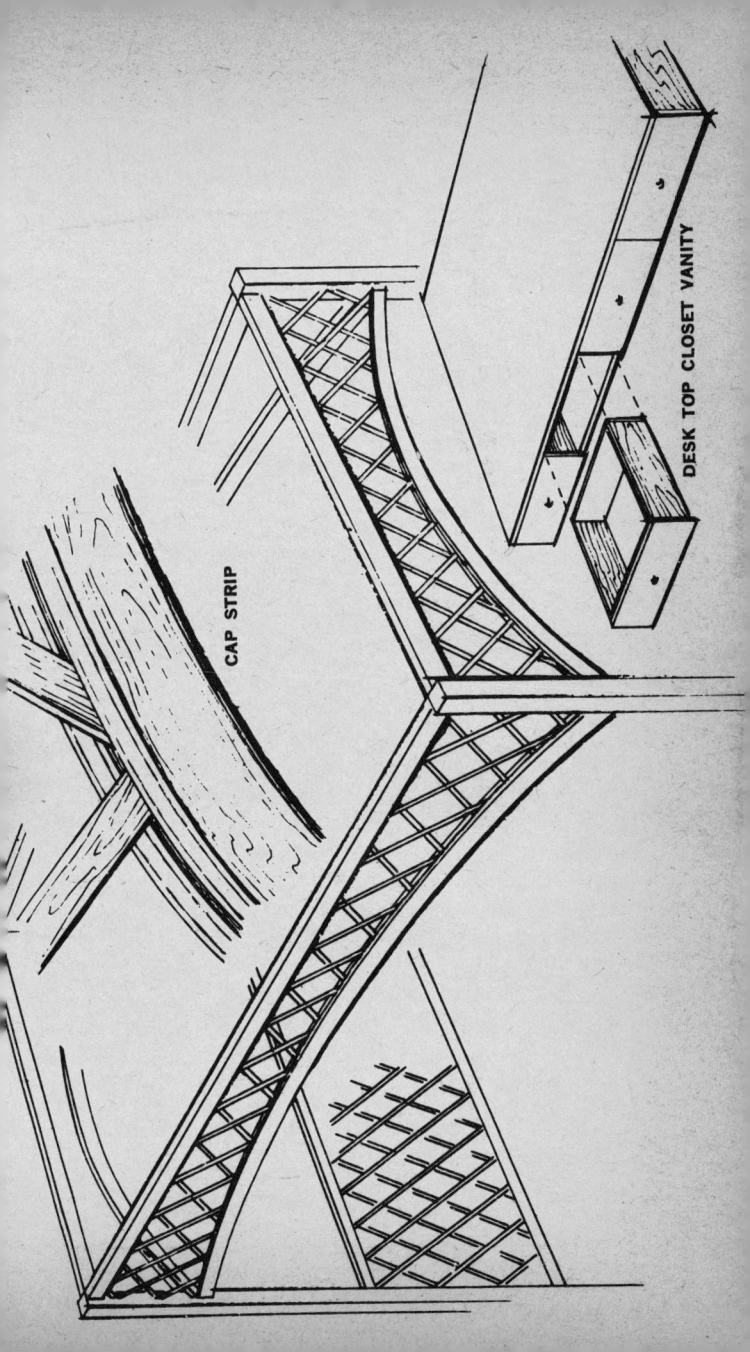

DESK TOP CLOSET VANITY

SPECIAL STORAGE IDEAS

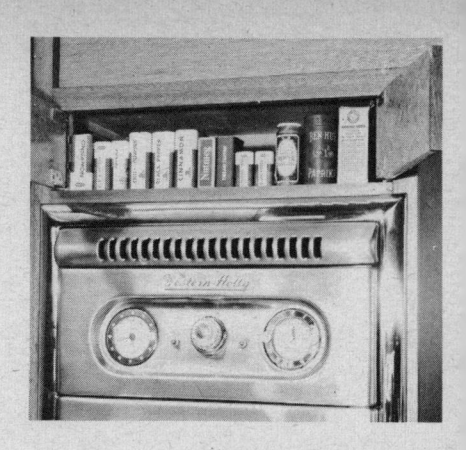

The pantry as a separate room for kitchen storage has given way to progress. Modern efficiency demands the carefully calculated utilization of every bit of space, as well as the convenience of storage close to point of preparation or use. This means finding space that might otherwise be overlooked, or the employment of special designs and hardware that permit the best possible usage of the space available. Shown here are some typical storage ideas for the kitchen that you might use or adapt to fit your own situation.

Photo at the top of the page shows a spice cupboard conveniently located in what would otherwise have been wasted space above a built-in oven. Upper illustration on the facing page shows a large step-saving drawer for storing oven utensils directly under the unit. Also, sliding, tiered drawer hardware can be utilized under the built-in range for easy access to range-top cooking tools.

In the lower photo a full-length cabinet has adjustable shelf brackets to take full advantage of available space.

A diligent search for storage space for small items immediately available to a specialized working area in your own kitchen can be surprisingly rewarding and mean a good deal more to the operational efficiency of the room than adding new equipment.

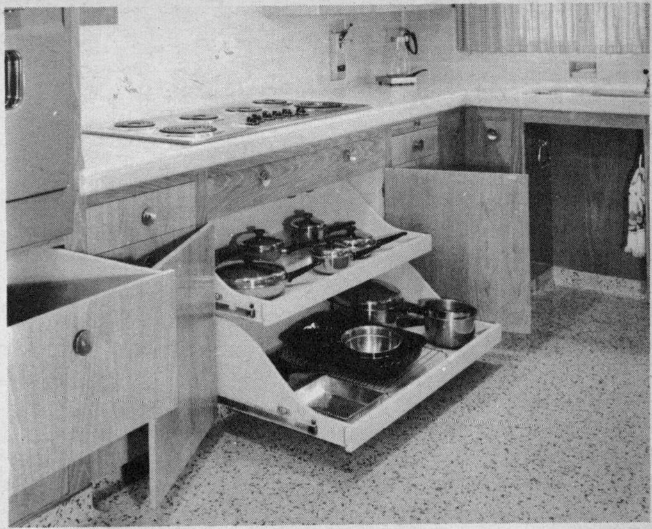

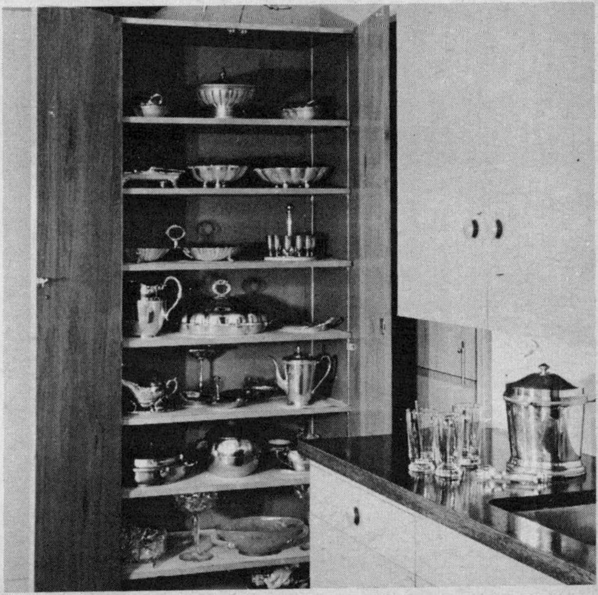

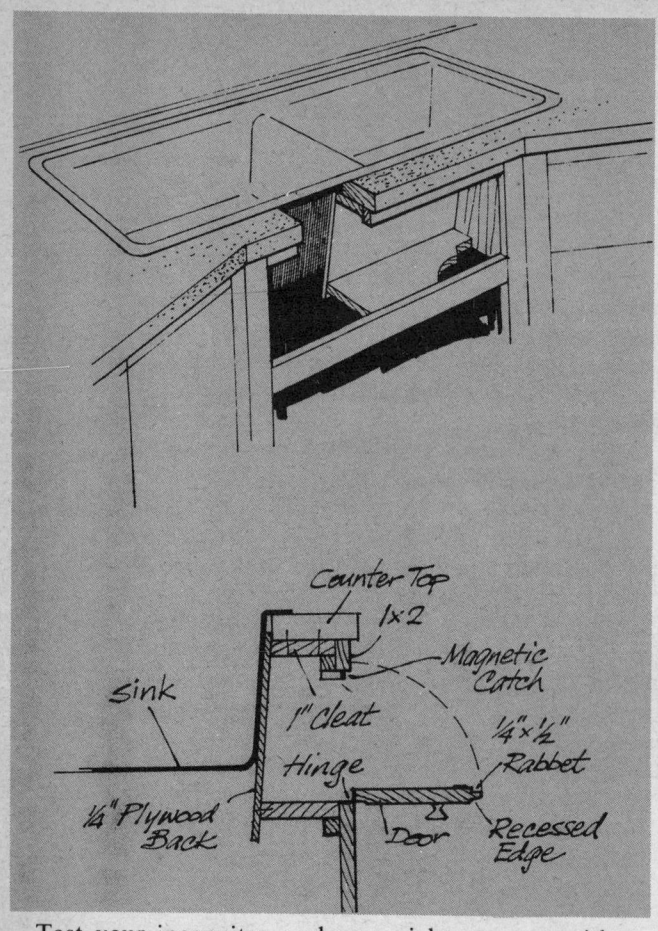

Test your ingenuity—and you might come up with an idea similar to the one shown in the diagram above. This homeowner discovered a handy and usually overlooked area between cabinet facing and countersunk kitchen sink for storing specialized items.

The framing detail and construction are self-explanatory. Just match hinges and hardware to the rest of the kitchen.

Tidiness is a kitchen quality sought by every housewife, and in this room perhaps more than any other there must be "a place for everything." The cabinet shown here utilizes simple shelves built right into the doors for convenient storage of awkwardly shaped items, while ample easy-to-reach shelf space is provided inside the cabinet for other kitchen utensils. Construction details are diagrammed above.

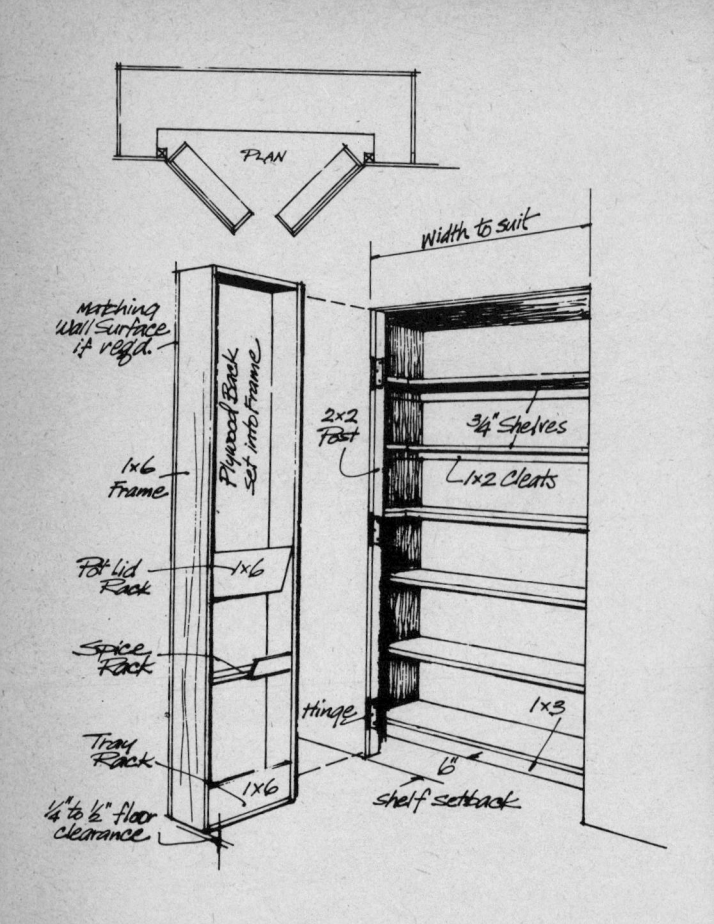

The overall dimensions of the unit are flexible—choose width, height and depth to suit your needs.

7 COUNTERTOPS
- A Vinyl Working Surface
- Vinyl Surface—The Easy Way
- A Mosaic Tile Top
- Plastic Laminate Surfaces
- A New Counter

A VINYL WORKING SURFACE

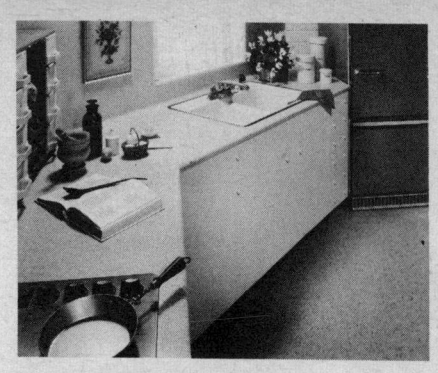

Careful planning of the kitchen layout is of utmost importance and proper lighting is probably equally so. But still another important factor is the choice of materials. This is especially true of the countertop working surfaces, which with the possible exception of the floor, take the worst beating in the modern kitchen.

Durability and ease of cleaning are essential here. Good looks are important, too.

Today the homeowner has at his disposal a wide choice of countertop materials in a great variety of decorative patterns. Best of all for the handyman, most of these materials are within the realm of the do-it-yourselfer. Shown on these pages are typical installations of three of the most popular—mosaic tiles, sheet vinyl, and laminated plastic.

Your choice of countertop may be governed by several factors—your personal aesthetics or sense of decor, ease of installation, maintenance performance or durability under hard usage. For simple, streamlined decor and maintenance it's hard to beat the flexible and virtually seamless vinyl installation shown above.

The countertop shown, along with backsplash and rolled edge, is cut from a single piece of sheet vinyl material. While this type of installation is fairly difficult, the experienced and dexterous handyman who takes his time and checks himself every step of the way should not find it too great a challenge, and the result will be a handsome working surface indeed. The procedure is described here. For those of you with more than the usual complement of thumbs, as well as others who just may prefer to do things the easy way, a more simplified method of installation is detailed later.

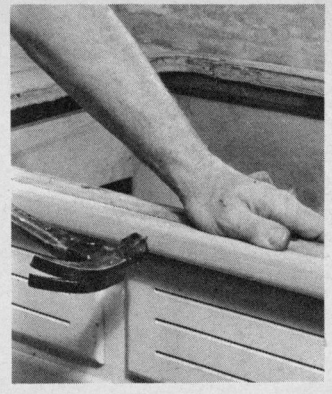

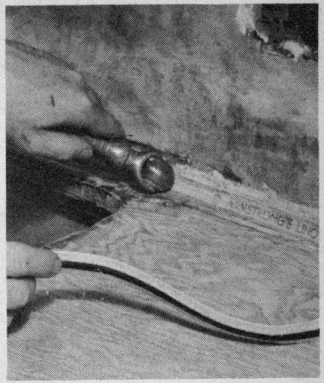

Your first step, of course, is the proper preparation of the surface to be covered. Fill all cracks and crevices and sand smooth. Next, cement and nail a dripless molding to the edge of the counter, as shown in left photo at the top of the page.

Cement is then applied at the wall-countertop joint and special fillet strip is carefully fitted into place to seal the joint against moisture (photo above at right).

Before starting to work with vinyl, make an exact pattern of the area to be covered, using a generous sheet of felt paper, as illustrated on the following page. The material is flexible, permitting you to make exact measurements around contours and for cutouts, and is available at most building materials stores and outlets.

You will find the time spent in making a mockup of your countertop and splashback rewarding in the final result achieved and in guarding against possibly costly miscalculations when you finally apply the vinyl.

Photo at the top (left) shows cutting and precise fitting of felt paper to the countertop. Hold it in place with thumbtacks and masking tape to prevent any shifting as you proceed. Carefully measure and mark key points for sink opening, range cutout, etc. on the felt paper, always checking preceding work as you go along (top right).

Scribe along all edges, around window sills, electrical outlets and so forth (above left), marking the pattern where the cuts are to be. Finally transfer marks from felt pattern to the vinyl material (right, above).

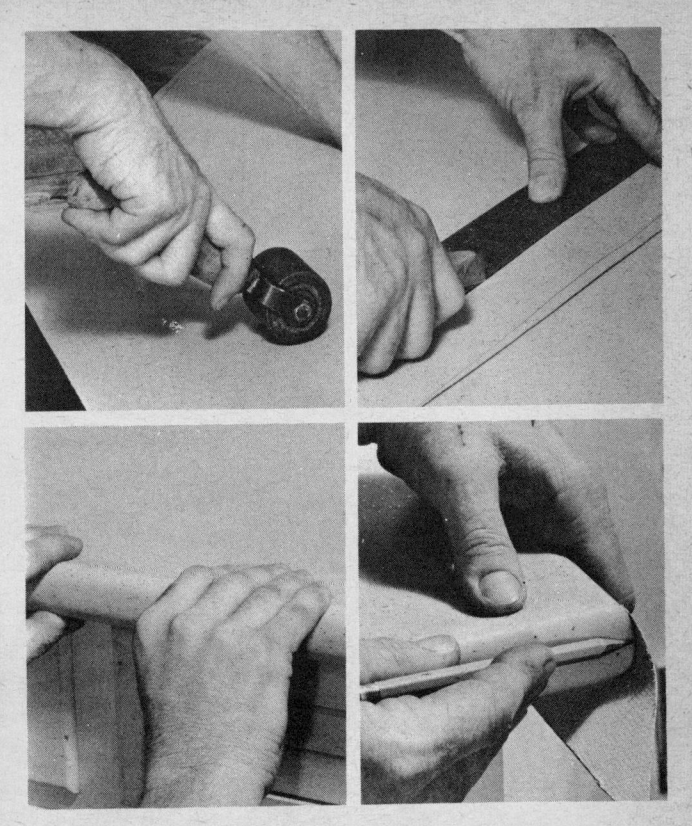

Allow adequate overlap at inside corners—excess is later cut. Cut the vinyl, apply cement to the countertop and splashback and smooth in place (photo at top left), using a hand roller for pressure. Overlapping material on the inside corner is double-cut (top, right) as soon as it is positioned, assuring perfect fit at this critical position.

Cement is applied to the back of the material at the roll edge—then this is carefully formed over the dripless molding for a finished edge (left, above). Outside corner of rolled edge is fitted by cutting to the corner, forming edge, marking edge against it, then trimming it, as shown in last photo on preceding page.

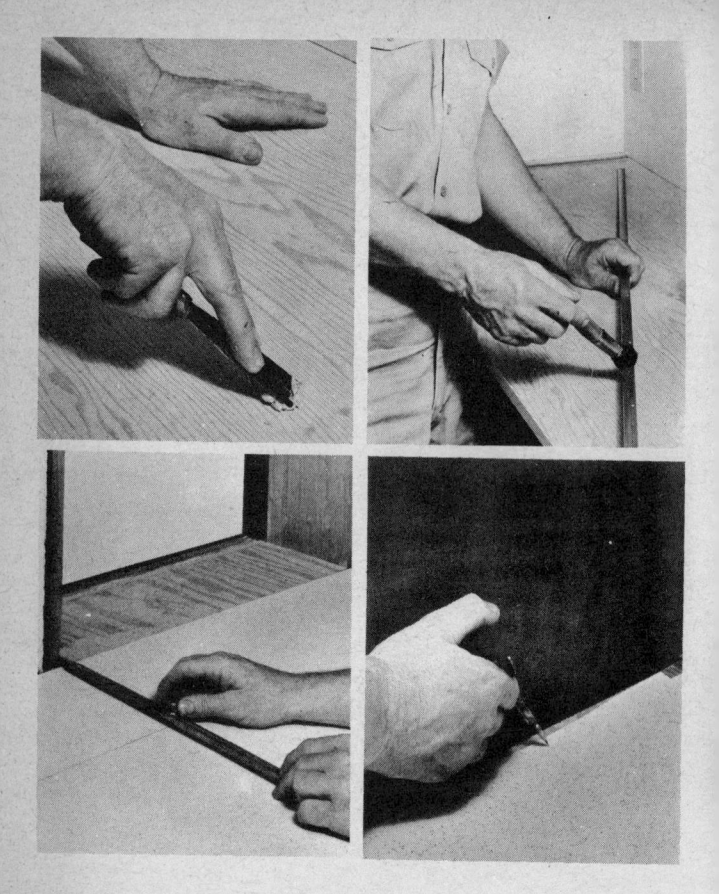

A simpler way—though perhaps not aesthetically pleasing in results—to vinyl-top your counter is illustrated in the photos on this and the facing page.

Start with surface preparation as before (top left photo), filling all cracks and joints and sanding smooth. The vinyl material is first installed on the wall. Then cove metal is fastened to the wall-countertop joint with contact cement (top right, preceding page). Next photo shows treatment of an offset—use scribing tool, scribe, then cut to fit. Butt the vinyl to the wall and use dividers (last photo on preceding page) to scribe along the wall for an accurate fit.

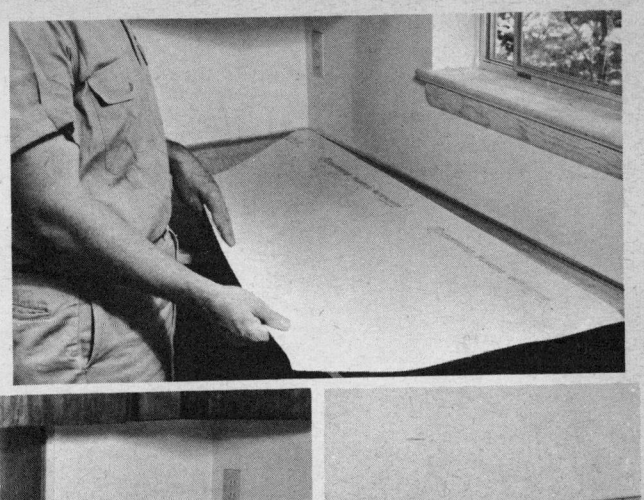

Cut the material. Apply cement to the counter and install the vinyl (photo at top). Smooth with a hand roller. Cut out the sink opening.

Illustrated above are two alternative edge treatments. Metal trim is used at left. Vinyl edging in the photo at right should be cemented in place before vinyl top is applied.

A MOSAIC TILE TOP

Effective, durable and easy to install, mosaic tile can give a specific working area in your kitchen a look of distinction. The slight additional attention required in maintenance by the grout between the tiles is more than repaid by the appearance and the varied effects obtainable —you're not likely to tire soon of the subtly shaded patterns.

The whole story is simply told in the five illustrations on this and the facing page. As shown in the photo above, cement is to be spread with a notched trowel and used generously.

Start with the wall. After applying the cement, set the sheet of tile in place and tap gently but firmly with a block of wood and hammer or a mallet, as shown in the top photo at right, to set the tiles evenly.

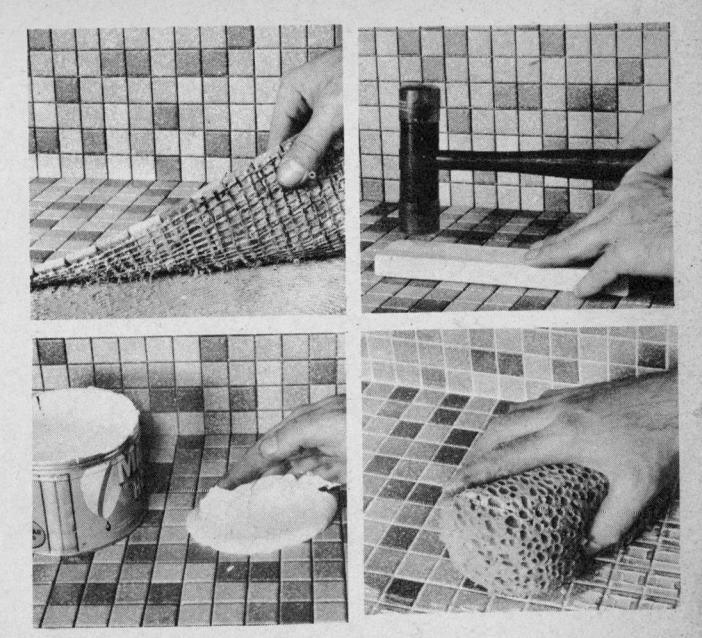

Match the countertop rows with those on the wall. Top left illustration shows webbed undersurface of the tile sheet—this permits the cement to penetrate upward and between the individual tiles—while holding the tiles together in perfect alignment—for firm bonding.

The next step in installation is to mix grout and spread it over the surface of the tiles, making sure that all the joints are filled. Then wipe grout off the face of the tiles with a wet sponge.

The tiles are easily cut or shaped—simply score with a fine saw and tap lightly with a hammer to break along the cut. Edges can be smoothed with a sander and concealed by butting against the wall-counter joint.

As in any project, careful planning and laying out the job before you start are important.

PLASTIC LAMINATE SURFACES

Plastic laminates are among the hardest, most durable materials made today for hard-working, maintenance-free countertops, come in a variety of colors and patterns to fit any decor and are available in rigid sheets of sufficiently varied sizes to enable you to plan fairly freely installations to suit your needs. Others come in flexible rolls up to forty feet in length for seamless installation on extra-long countertops.

Shown on this and the next two pages are relatively simple steps for covering existing surfaces—the same basic rules apply to more elaborate counter remodeling jobs, to be dealt with later.

Laminated plastic should be installed over smooth, clean surface. Contact cement is spread over countertop, as shown above, and over the back of the plastic sheet. It is allowed to dry to the touch. Plastic is then applied and pressed firmly into place using a roller (photo at top left, facing page). Excess material is trimmed off with a sharp file as illustrated at top right. Metal molding is installed in the cove and the backsplash strip is set in place (middle photo at right). Metal edge stripping completes installation, as at left center.

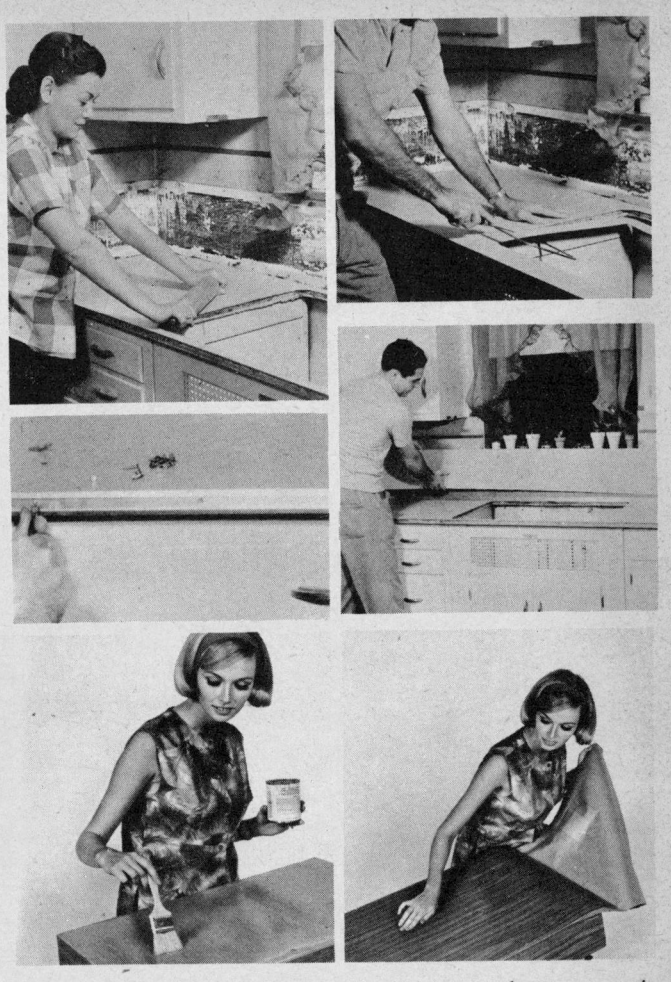

The flexibility of the plastic laminate that comes in rolls can be an aid to the do-it-yourself mechanic. The young lady shown above is covering a small tabletop. Installation procedure would be the same for a kitchen counter. Contact adhesive is applied to both the laminate and the surface to be covered and allowed to dry tacky. A slipsheet of kraft paper is laid over the surface, then the laminate is set in place as the slip sheet is withdrawn as shown in last photo on preceding page.

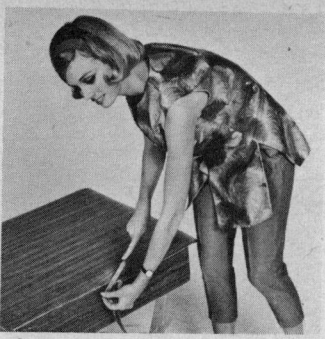

A roller is used to work out any air bubbles and achieve permanent contact (left, above). The edge of a fine-tooth file is used to cut the overlapping material and to make neat, square edges (above, right).

But suppose you want to do more than merely recover an already existing countertop with plastic laminate. Any number of reasons may exist for replacing the entire kitchen counter. Because it's worn, or because you're replacing or refinishing your cabinets, or perhaps because you want to add some new dimension to the decor of your kitchen. Whatever your objective, you can now do a job that's the equal of any coming out of a professional shop. It just takes a little know-how.

The new counter described on the following pages consists, basically, of plastic laminate bonded to a base. The simplest way is to build the complete top as a separate unit, then put in place.

First remove the existing countertop, leaving the tops of the cabinets exposed. If the counter has a sink, both it and the faucets must be disconnected and removed.

Next, measure for the size top you'll need. The standard countertop overhang is ¾ inch. As a general rule kitchen base cabinets are 23 inches deep, so when you halve a standard 4-foot-wide sheet or core material you will have pieces just about the right depth for this overhang.

The base can be exterior grade plywood or flakeboard. Until the last few years, plywood was the standard coring material for countertops. In recent years, however, flakeboard products have been steadily gaining in popularity. Cost differential between the two is negligible, and each has its advantages. Flakeboard is more stable than plywood and is less inclined to warp. But it's also considerably heavier, and large pieces therefore more difficult to handle.

Laminates usually come in sheets a few inches larger than standard 4 x 8-foot (or 4 x 10 or 4 x 12, etc.) panels to allow for the edge trimming that's necessary. As you calculate how much material you'll need, avoid joints as much as possible by using the longest lengths available. For instance, if you are going to build an 11 ½-foot-long top, buy 12-foot lengths of core and laminate rather than joining an 8-foot piece with a 3 ½-footer. If the countertop has to turn a corner, you'll probably have to join pieces.

When measuring, check the corners of the walls for squareness, wherever the end of the top butts against it. Even in new houses, corners and walls are not always perfectly square. For a professional job, the top will have to fit precisely. So, if necessary, trim the coring to fit.

Now that you have your materials, the exact dimensions and angles, you're ready to build the top. As mentioned, halve your sheet of core material into two 24-inch-wide lengths (assuming your cabinets are 23-inches deep). You can do this on a table saw, with a portable circular saw, or have it done by the lumberyard where you purchase the coring. If you do your own cutting, be sure of two things. First, use a good, sharp, fine-tooth plywood blade. This leaves a nice smooth edge. Second, make sure your cut is absolutely straight. You are going to be cutting a big chunk of heavy, cumbersome material and even with a bench saw it is all too easy to come up with a wavy cut—and a sloppy-looking top. Get someone to help you handle the piece while you're cutting it.

Next, cut the core material to length. Set the core in place on the cabinets and make sure it fits perfectly.

The standard thickness for a laminated counter top is 2½ inches. Since the core material is only ¾-inch thick, you build it up with ¾-inch strips of some of the cut offs, as illustrated, top left photo on the facing page. Cut two strips of coring two to three inches wide and the same length as the top. Glue, nail or screw these along the front and rear edges on the bottom (unfinished side if you're using plywood) making the outer edges of the strips and the main piece flush. Then do the same at each end. If a sink will be in the top, also add a strip on each side of where it will be, allowing clearance for the sink cut-out. For extra strength on a long top, it's a good idea to fasten several additional crosspieces between the perimeter frame, placed at points where they will locate against the tops of the cabinet partitions.

To insure smooth, square edges it's best to run over those which will laminate with either a power plane or a belt sander.

Now you're ready to start the laminating and you begin with the edges. First the exposed ends, then the front edge and last the top. Same order for the splashboard.

Cut the laminate to size, allowing at least ½-inch, preferably more, waste on the edges.

It's best to cut laminate with a table saw (face down) or radial arm saw (face up). Use an old, fine-tooth plywood blade or if you don't have an old one, buy a cheap one. Plastic laminate is pretty tough stuff; once you've used a blade on it, it isn't much good for anything else. Also be sure to wear goggles while cutting. The chips are hard and really fly.

The laminate is bonded to the core with contact cement. There are many good brands on the market. I have become partial to the new waterbase types because they aren't flammable and don't smell as bad as the old types.

Before you begin, make sure the cement is well-mixed, particularly the water-based type. Don't rely on merely shaking the can. Stir it thoroughly with a stick and use a work area where the temperature is above 65 degrees. For best results avoid working on materials that have been stored in a cold place. Both core and laminate should be 65 degrees or warmer. Make sure they're free of oil, grit or dirt, too.

Now, apply a good, heavy coat of cement to both the core and the laminate, as shown above. A clean paint brush will do or, for big areas, you can use a paint roller. When you apply the cement, brush or roll in *one direction* only. Don't work it back and forth as you would paint. Drying time varies, depending on the type of cement and other factors such as humidity and temperature. It's usually about 20 to 30 minutes. Check for proper dryness by pressing a piece of paper against the coated surface, then pulling it off. The paper should stick slightly, but none of the cement should come away with it. One good coat is usually sufficient, although core edges often soak up the adhesive and a second coat is in order.

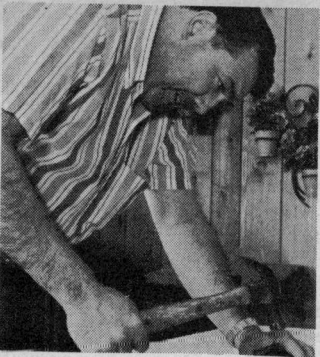

Now comes the part where most first-timers run into trouble—applying the laminate to the core. Once the laminate touches the core, the contact cement grabs tenaciously and holds it fast. If it's improperly aligned, you're out of luck. To avoid crooked placement, cover the core with sheets of heavy kraft paper, carefully putting the laminate in its correct position on the paper. Once everything is lined up, slowly slip the paper out, pressing the laminate down with the heel of your hand at the same time.

To complete the bond, tap the laminate with a small block of scrap wood and a mallet—see photos above. Cover the entire area. This is very important for the strongest possible bond.

Trim the edges as you go. There are several tools for this. You can rent a laminate trimmer (a small, router-like gadget made especially for the purpose) or you can use a regular router either equipped with a special base plate and adjustable guide, illustrated in action on the facing page.

Or for even easier trimming, get hold of one of the new low-priced router bits with a built-in guide. You will need two bits—one for straight cuts, one for bevels.

The actual trimming is a snap. Just set the depth so that the cutter is level with the edge of the laminate. The guide rides along the edge of the core material and the cutter trims the laminate flush. There is one thing to watch out for if you are using plywood for a core: there may be some holes in the edges from open knots. Should these be in the path of the pilot, it could drop into one and ruin your cut. If you see any holes, go by them freehand, leaving a little extra laminate, then trim this section by hand with a fine-mill file.

Just follow the same procedure with each part, including the backsplash. The backsplash is simply a double thickness of coring, two to three inches high and the same length as the top. Use the straight cutter for all edges which will butt up against another piece of laminate and bevel the rest.

When all of the surfaces have been laminated, clamp the backsplash to the top and fasten it with long wood screws (see photo at right, above), driven up through the underside of the top and go through it into the backsplash.

If you have two sections to join, you can use a special-purpose fastener called a "Tight-Joint." As shown in the photo on the following page, all it involves is butting the two sections to be joined, drilling holes in core strips on the edge of each section, using fastener guide as illustrated at top left, then slipping in and tightening up the fasteners to join the sections (photo at top right). Complete instructions come with the fastener.

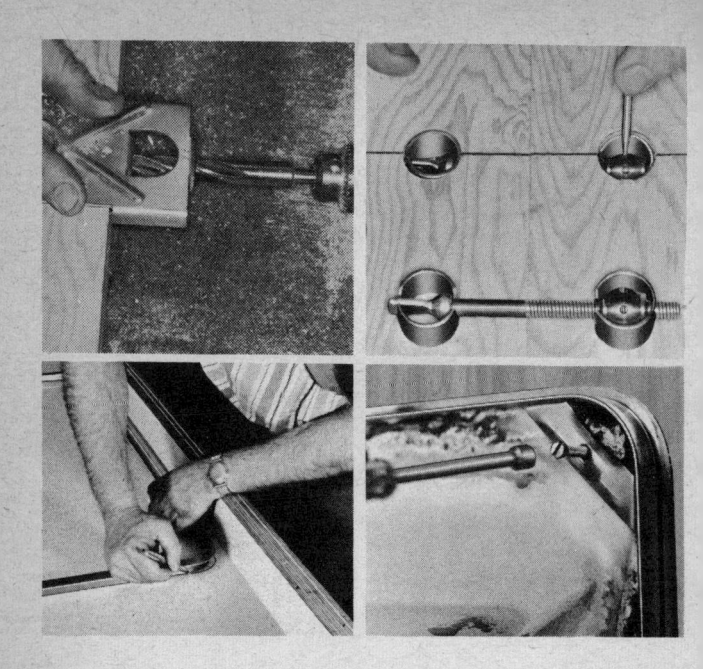

Locate the position of the sink and use the new rim as a guide for the cutout (left photo, above). Just place the rim on the top and outline it with a grease pencil, then make the cutout with a sabre saw equipped with a fine-tooth, metal-cutting blade.

Now you can position the top in place and fasten it with small angle brackets attached to the bottom of the countertop and the tops of the cabinet partitions.

Mounting the sink is simple. Calk the inside of the rim, fit it on the sink and secure it with the corner clips provided and shown in photo at right, above. Apply more calk to the countertop side of the rim, then place the sink in the cutout and draw it secure with the mounting clips.

8 LAUNDRIES
- **Plan a Kitchen Laundry Center**
- **Folding Doors to Conceal a Laundry Center**

PLAN A KITCHEN LAUNDRY CENTER

While more home laundries are still located in basements than in any other area of the home, the trend is growing toward other, more convenient locations. According to a recent survey by a leading appliance manufacturer, about one in three purchasers of automatic washers placed their laundry areas in the basement. The same study showed about 25 per cent of new automatic washers placed in the kitchen.

The kitchen is particularly practical for the homemaker who makes this room her headquarters. With automatic laundry equipment, little time or attention is required and the task can be interspersed with other activities. Like other first-floor locations, the kitchen laundry is usually within easy access of the telephone, the front door and the children in the yard. A utility room off the kitchens won't accomodate laundry equipment. Even small areas such as pantries, hallways and closets may offer solutions to serious space problems. A space as small as five feet wide is sufficient, provided there are facilities for sorting, pretreating and storing soiled clothes and laundry supplies.

However cramped or poorly laid out, the first-floor laundry has an important advantage over its basement counterpart. It is near the other work areas, the source of the soiled laundry and storage for clean laundry. Taking the "transportation" out of laundering has long been a goal of homemakers and home economists.

Space is, of course, a prime factor. The drawing and floor plan shown above illustrate how a laundry area may be fitted into a small kitchen.

There should definitely be a separation between the food preparation area and the laundry area, as well as plenty of storage. Without storage for soiled clothes and laundry supplies, the kitchen will seldom look spic-and-span.

You may wish to make provisions for closing off the laundry when not in use. Folding doors are often the answer here and will be detailed later for adaptation by the do-it-yourselfer.

It takes more than a convenient location and a washer and dryer to make a workable laundry center. The allotment of space, based on size of appliances, necessary working room and direction of work-flow, should be the first consideration.

Shown above is a space-saver—a stacked washer and dryer. The unit can wash over twelve pounds of clothing in the washer below while twelve pounds is being dried above. The unit fits flush against the wall, features storage space and can be built next to your kitchen office area—of which more will be said later—permitting you to use the time while the unit is at work to other advantage. The arrangement shown also features accessibility to outdoors and light chores there.

Another idea is to combine your kitchen laundry with a cozy breakfast nook, as shown on the facing page, blending the decor with that of the rest of your kitchen. Note also the island sink serving both the laundry and kitchen areas.

In fact, the possibilities of adding to the effectiveness of your day with a kitchen-laundry combination are endless. If your layout permits, think and plan beyond the obvious step-saving advantages of the arrangement—break down your whole working schedule to its time-components and consider the whole while laying out your plans. Priorities apply—but any time and labor-saving device or arrangement is doubly effective if the time and the labor saved can be put to some other equally necessary use.

Illustrated on the next two pages are kitchen-laundry combinations that present multiple advantages. The layout shown on the following pages not only incorporates the kitchen-office area with the laundry but also includes a play area for toddlers adjacent to both kitchen and laundry, thereby adding a definite safety factor to the effective operation of your household.

In this arrangement Mom can keep an eye on the children from the kitchen or when she is at the laundry center or planning her day at the "office."

The arrangement also incorporates a strategic placement of the office area: Mom is right in the center of things, in the middle of the action, as it were, a few steps away from the kitchen, which is also in operation, while the safety gate keeps child from potential mischief and possible danger.

The kitchen on the facing page is arranged to combine meal preparation, eating and laundry facilities within easy reach of each other. While it is designed primarily to offer suggestions for remodeling a big kitchen, many of the features it contains can be applied to smaller kitchens.

Note the abundance of cabinet space—this is an idea that can be applied anywhere. The partition that separates the kitchen and laundry areas contains open shelves and serve-through space. This enables quick meals to be served easily through to the eating bar on the other side of the partition. The wall opening also makes it easy to keep an eye on the laundry operations while kitchen work is being done. The "office" is placed at the end of the partition, so that planning can be done with the whole field of operations clearly in view.

The minimum laundry requirements are:

- Laundry equipment—washer and dryer or combination washer dryer
- Storage for soiled clothes, preferably at least three bins for sorting by laundry loads

- Storage for laundry aids—detergent, bleach, etc.
- Space for sorting, folding, pre-treating (could be tops of appliances).

Optimum laundry center would include:

- Laundry equipment—washer and dryer or combination washer-dryer
- Space to store soiled clothes, sorted by type of load—six bins: three large, three small
- Place to store laundry aids (should include stain removal kit, with storage out of reach of children but convenient to homemaker)
- Space to sort and fold clothes: pre-ironing storage of clean clothes
- Provision for ironing and storage of iron, board, etc.
- Provision for hanging clothing removed from dryer
- Provision for sewing, or at least mending

Appliances, plumbing electricity conform to sufficiently general standards for you to pre-plan accurately.

A washer and dryer together require approximately five feet of wall space. The depth of most appliances, including combinations, is about 28 inches. To this should be added from 36 to 42 inches of floor space for adequate working room.

The two illustrations on the facing page show how separation of laundry and kitchen areas was accomplished in crowded quarters without sacrifice of proper operating area. In the top photo the washer was isolated from the kitchen appliances by simply turning its back to them and, incidentally, to the view from the dinette.

In the lower photo folding wood doors (to be detailed later, on page 136) conceal the laundry center when it is not in operation.

The washer will, of course, require hot and cold water taps with an outlet for the drain. Most dryers should be vented to the outside. About 30 feet of venting (no elbows) is maximum for efficient operation. Each elbow reduces this figure by 4 feet (i.e., maximum efficiency with 1 elbow is 26 feet, with elbows 22 feet, etc.). A no-vent dryer, usually requiring a cold water tap and a drain, provides a solution to the venting problem.

Gas dryers naturally will require a gas supply. All gas dryers need venting.

A nearby sink is convenient for pre-treating heavily soiled laundry, stain removal, starching, and filling the sprinkler attachment of a dryer. If the laundry area is at one end of the kitchen, it may be possible to locate an island sink as a divider between the two areas.

All electric washers require a standard 115-volt circuit. In addition, electric dryers should have a 230-volt circuit. Although many dryers can operate on a 115-volt circuit, drying time is increased. Gas dryers require 115-volt.

The laundry area needs good general lighting, plus specific illumination for pre-treating, mending and ironing centers.

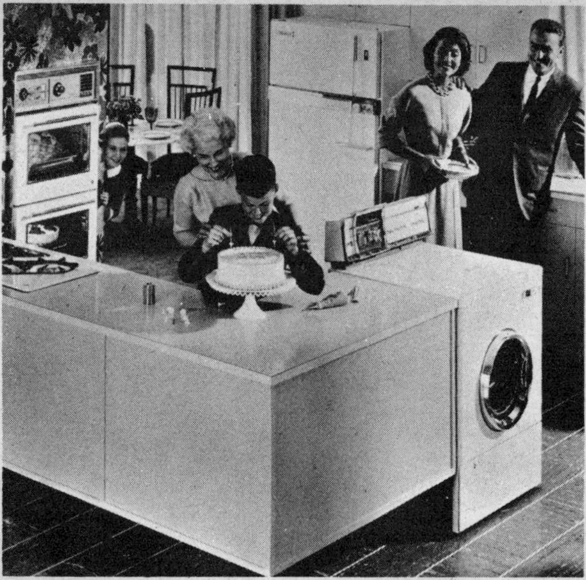

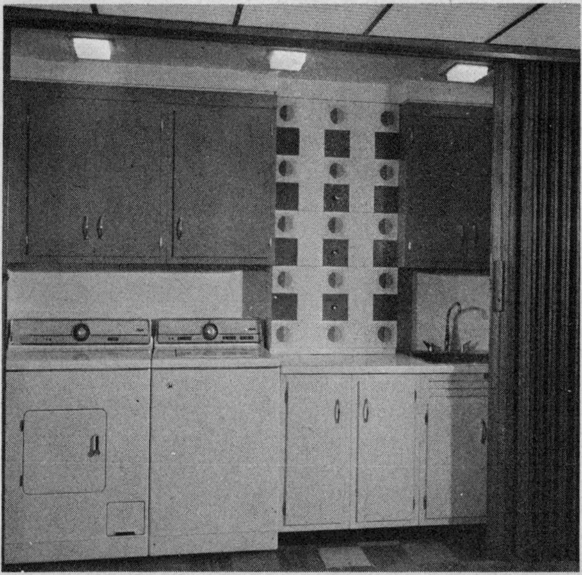

A variety of drawers, shelves, cabinets and closets is necessary for storage of soiled clothes, laundry supplies and clean laundry preparatory to ironing and/or mending. Soiled clothes storage is probably the most important and most frequently overlooked aspect of good laundry planning. Different washables require different laundering "recipes" and shouldn't be washed together. Any given armload of soiled laundry might contain items for two or three different washer loads, and a place to pre-sort and store these items within the laundry area is essential. The trend toward doing a load or two of laundry each day rather than doing it all on one day intensifies this need. Dumping everything into a single bin would mean dumping it all out and sorting every time a washload is selected.

Everything washable can be broken down into approximately six categories. However, not every home will contain a substantial amount of each of these categories, or perhaps space limitations will not permit this large a storage area, so three, four or five separate bins may be adequate. The minimum for effective storage is three—one for white loads, another for colored items and a third for specials. Bin sizes can vary, too, with the white loads normally largest in most homes and the basic colored loads probably next.

The type of container can also vary considerably. Perhaps undercounter bins can be built in, or large drawers. Laundry baskets on shelves or even on the floor in an out-of-the-way place could do the trick. Whatever is used, allowances for adequate ventilation should be made.

Using this pre-sorting system, whenever a container is full enough for a washer load, it can be put into the washer.

Aids for good laundering have come a long way since the days of bar soap, bleach and ammonia. They now are both more effective and more numerous, and adequate space is needed for handy storage near the washer or sink, if one is available. Some overhead storage is desirable to eliminate stooping, while some undercounter space is needed for extra-large boxes of detergent or heavy bottles of bleach.

The laundry equipment shown in the corner installation above has been designed to fit standard cabinet dimensions shown at left leading to the business part of the kitchen, and providing under-the-counter storage permitting separation of items. This installation also provides hobby time in an indoor garden. The overhead storage shown can be adapted for laundry items, hobby utensils—or used for both.

Tied closely to laundering aids but worthy of special mention are items for pre-treating and stain removal, such as acetone, glycerine, ammonia, color remover, etc. Good laundry practice still requires pre-treating. A sink is handy for this and for other uses. A cup and brush are convenient in pre-treating and a drawer, preferably near the sink, is a good spot to store them, as well as other useful items.

A load of clothes coming out of the dryer demands space for folding and sorting. A good idea is to remove items from the dryer one at a time, fold each one and make piles according to where the clean clothes are to go. If sufficient counter space is not available for this job, you might consider a shelf above the laundry equipment for temporarily piling up folded items to put away. The washer and dryer tops themselves provide space for folding.

Another helpful idea, space permitting, is to provide separate trays or baskets for each family member, into which to place socks and underwear, for instance. Then each one has the responsibility to see that these items get back where they belong.

Almost as big a problem as what to do with soiled clothes is the one presented when a load of fresh, clean clothes has come from the dryer. Some of the items in the load will have to go somewhere to await ironing, other things may need mending before being used again, everything else needs to be folded and eventually returned to its storage location. A hamper for things to be ironed is helpful in maintaining order in the laundry area.

Proper location can be a step-saver here, too. Just as clothes must be collected for laundering, they must be returned afterward. If linen storage, for instance, can be located handy to the laundry area, the increased convenience will be significant. A horizontal pass-through can also be helpful. For example, an overhead cabinet in the laundry area might also open into an adjoining bathroom or hall for convenient storage of towels or linens. Remember that every step saved in the laundry procedure will be saved many, many times.

The ideal place to handle the ironing chore is at the laundry center. This means space for an ironing board—about four by six feet—plus convenient storage for the board and iron. An asbestos plate for the iron in its storage location will eliminate the need to let it stand out to cool.

Don't forget a place to hang things as they are ironed. It might range from a wall hook to a handy, full-length closet in the laundry area. This hanging space is also needed when wash-and-wear items are removed from the dryer, so it is well to locate it near the dryer where possible. If a closet, it might be a good spot to store the ironing board when not in use.

Laundry time is the time to check articles for needed mending. Often this should be done before things are washed, so tears don't get any larger. Hence, at least a space for mending supplies should be included in the laundry center. Often, it can be a place for other sewing as well. This provides an excellent secondary use for space devoted to the laundry center.

Thus far we have discussed the ideal laundry center—even if space allowed only a minimum ideal. But perhaps you live in a home or apartment with a kitchen (or other available laundry area) so small that even this minimum laundry center is beyond attainment. The wash is still going to have to be done and, if those all-too-frequent trips to a crowded self-service laundry are to be avoided, you will simply have to settle for less than the ideal.

There are available portable automatic washers that are only two feet wide, can be stored wherever convenient, and, when washday comes, can be rolled up to the kitchen sink, attached to the faucet and filled with a full-sized load of laundry. The casters on these units can be raised or lowered as needed so that they sit solidly on the floor when in use, then roll quickly out of the way.

Sorting, drying and folding are other problems, of course, but with ingenuity you can solve these. The old clothes line is still available, and the kitchen table will do in a pinch for sorting and folding (with careful scheduling). Hardly the ideal arrangements, but they will serve, if necessary, until something better can be worked out.

Thus, there is a strong case for locating the laundry area in or near the kitchen, and you should give serious thought to this possibility as part of your kitchen remodeling program. For convenience and efficiency, it's hard to beat, but careful planning is essential.

If you'd like to have the convenience and other benefits of a laundry center in your kitchen—but don't cotton to the idea of having it look like a laundry center—all you need is some otherwise wasted kitchen wall space and you can have it by adopting or adapting the idea shown on page 131. The washing machine and dryer are placed in a handy recess enclosed by folding doors. When laundry equipment is idle, the doors conceal it.

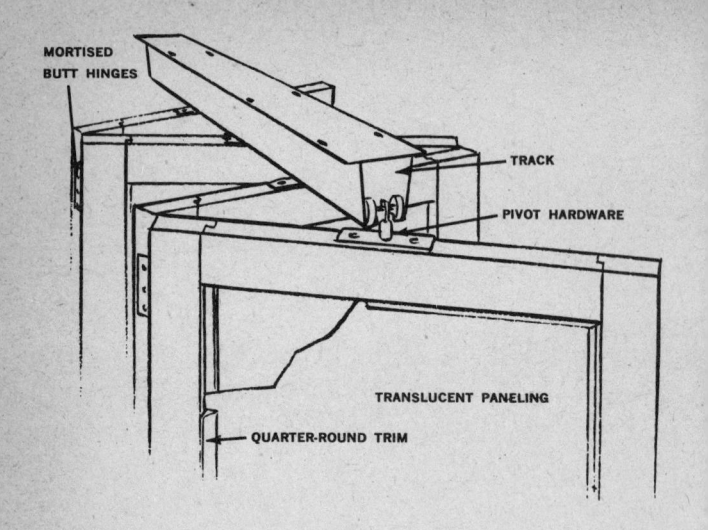

Many kinds of folding door hardware are available. This type requires only an overhead track, diagrammed above.

The door panels can be bought ready-made at most lumberyards or, if you prefer to show off your skills, it is not difficult to put them together from pre-cut molding. The paneling within the frame is a translucent Formica product called Walden (see What It's Called and Where to Buy It, page 189). Make as many panels as you need. Build high enough to fit the opening and adjust the width so that all are equal. Join with small hinges at top, bottom and center between each pair.

9 CLOSETS
- **More Use From Your Closets**
- **Closet-on-a-Door**
- **Utility Closet**

MORE
USE FROM YOUR CLOSETS

There is probably not a house in the land that couldn't use more storage space, but when existing facilities are taxed to the limit and additional needs develop, finding new places for more things can be exasperating. Observation, planning and careful organization are the keys to the problem.

The photo above shows a kitchen cabinet which has been well organized to provide places for cooking tools, pots, lids and so on. Spoon racks can be made to your own requirements, with as many cutouts as needed. Be sure to leave enough space between cutouts to permit free access to each tool. The sides of the pot lid racks and bag boxes on the doors are made from 1x4 to 1x2 stock, and the fronts from any available material; for example, hardboard, or ¼- or 3/8-inch plywood.

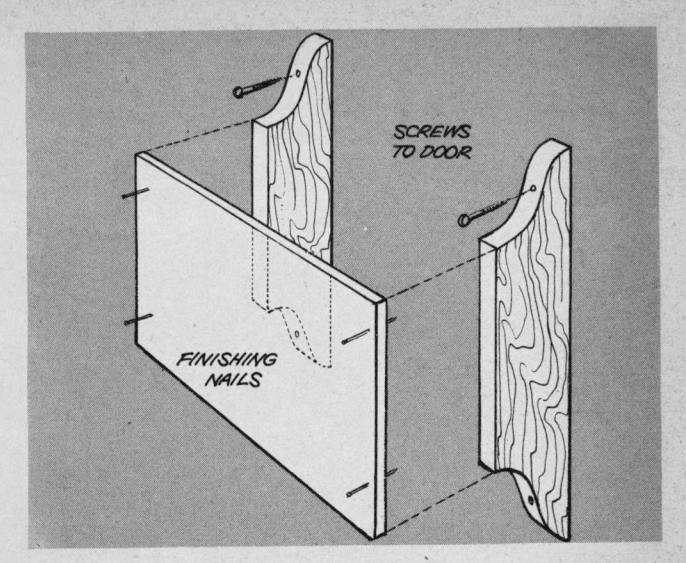

Simple construction diagrams for the pot lid racks and bag boxes are shown on above and on the following page. Cut the sides of the pot lid racks as shown simultaneously —clamp two pieces of 1 x 4 together and use a jigsaw— for uniformity of shape. Drill holes and screw to the door, using either roundhead screws or countersinking flatheads and filling over the holes. Use either finishing nails or countersunk screws to fasten the fronts to the sides.

For spoon and ladle racks use 1x2 stock. Drill holes, centering them about three inches apart, to accept the handles of the items to be stored—1" diameter holes are recommended—and saw cutouts in front for easy removal. Screw to back wall at a height that will not interfere with the door racks.

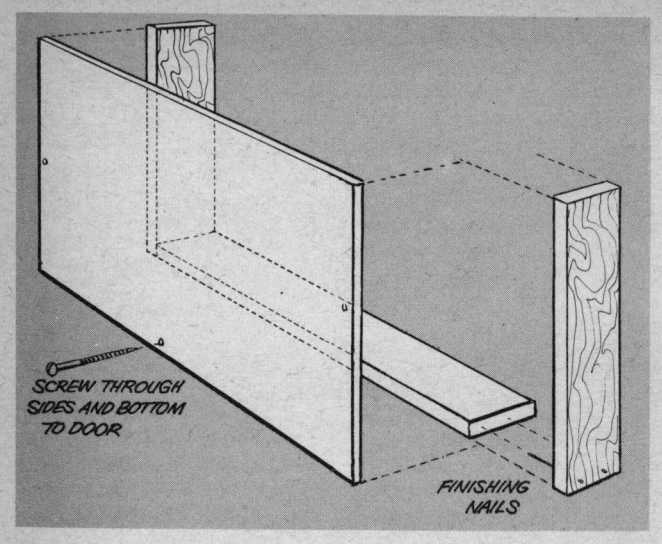

Make the side pieces and bottom of the bag racks as shown above from 1x2 stock and fasten together with either flathead screws or finishing nails. Drill holes through the front piece, bottom and sides as shown in the diagram and use long screws through all four pieces to secure the unit to the door.

In most cabinets there is at least one surface that is not being used to its fullest capacity. It could be a partition wall, the floor, the bottom of a shelf—even the ceiling. Don't let these useful areas stand idle while you fret over your quandary.

In the photo on the facing page an idle wall has been made to do yeoman service for storing vacuum cleaner accessories. Brushes and fittings hang on short 1-inch dowels glued to a piece of 2x4 which may be cut to any shape. The one shown is convenient, for it is easily fastened to the wall by a single screw through a hole drilled in the thin lower part. Make as many hangers as you need from whatever stock you happen to have.

The hose hanger can be cut to almost any dimension.

2 × 4 STOCK

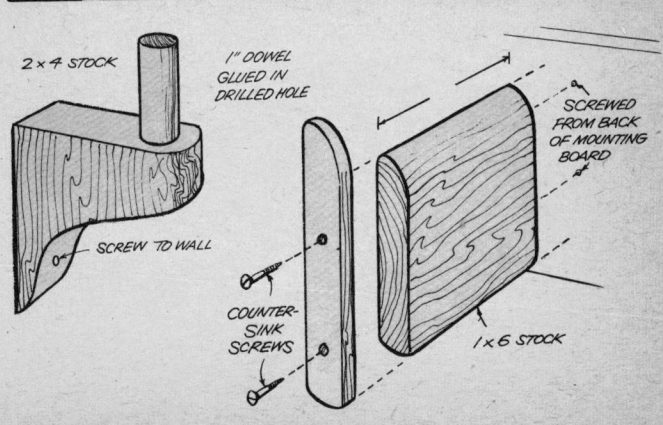

1" DOWEL GLUED IN DRILLED HOLE

SCREWED FROM BACK OF MOUNTING BOARD

SCREW TO WALL

COUNTER-SINK SCREWS

1 × 6 STOCK

CLOSET-ON-A-DOOR

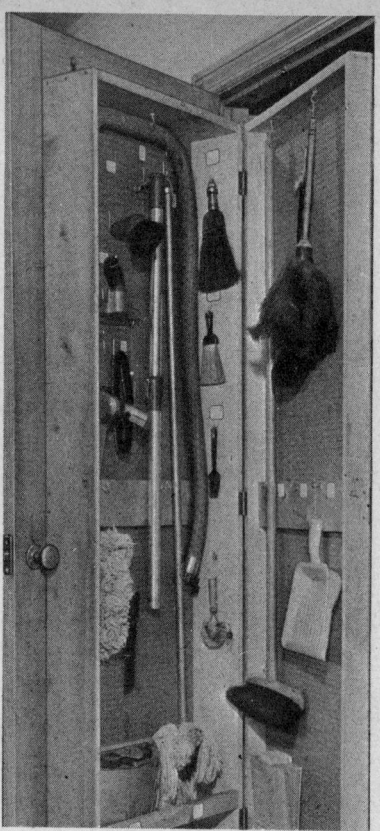

Above you see an open and shut case. If you have to climb over an untidy pile of mops, brooms and miscellaneous cleaning tools every time you're basement-bound, lose no time in cleaning it up. If it remains, sooner or later someone will be in too great a hurry to be wary, and a serious fall down the stairs could result.

You need not take up valued closet space for the purpose—nor do you have to store the tools unhandily in the basement. Seen here, in photographs taken at the home of Mr. and Mrs. A. Pilpel of Valley Stream, N.Y., is an ingenious on-the-door closet for mops, brushes and brooms. There's even room for a carpet sweeper and assorted vacuum cleaner attachments.

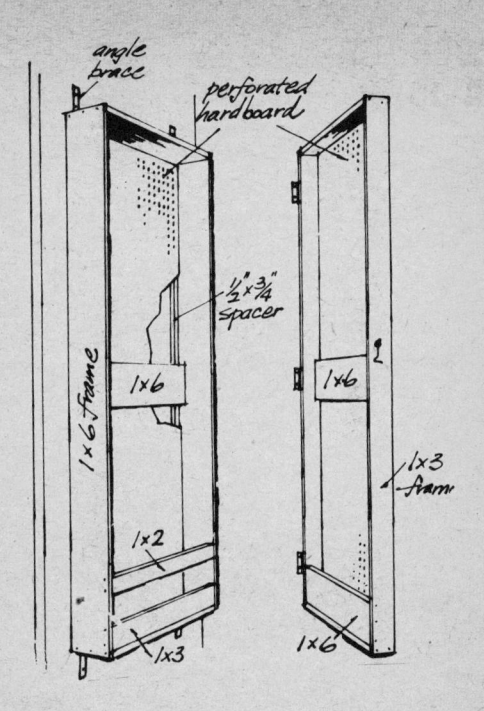

With the exception of the perforated hardboard that provides the place to 'plug in' hooks from which the tools hang, the closet can be built from odds and ends. If you have to purchase the materials, you won't spend more than a few dollars.

Dimensions are made as large as may be permitted by the door you are going to use as a base. Make suitable box frame of 1x6 stock and fasten it to the back of the main door with angle braces top and bottom. The hardboard panel is screwed to ½ x ¾" spacers. The "door" to the closet is a 1x3 frame backed up by another perforated hardboard panel screwed to it. Nail in the 1x6 cross braces and hang the completed door on butt hinges. A screw-eye and hook keeps it closed when not in use.

UTILITY CLOSET

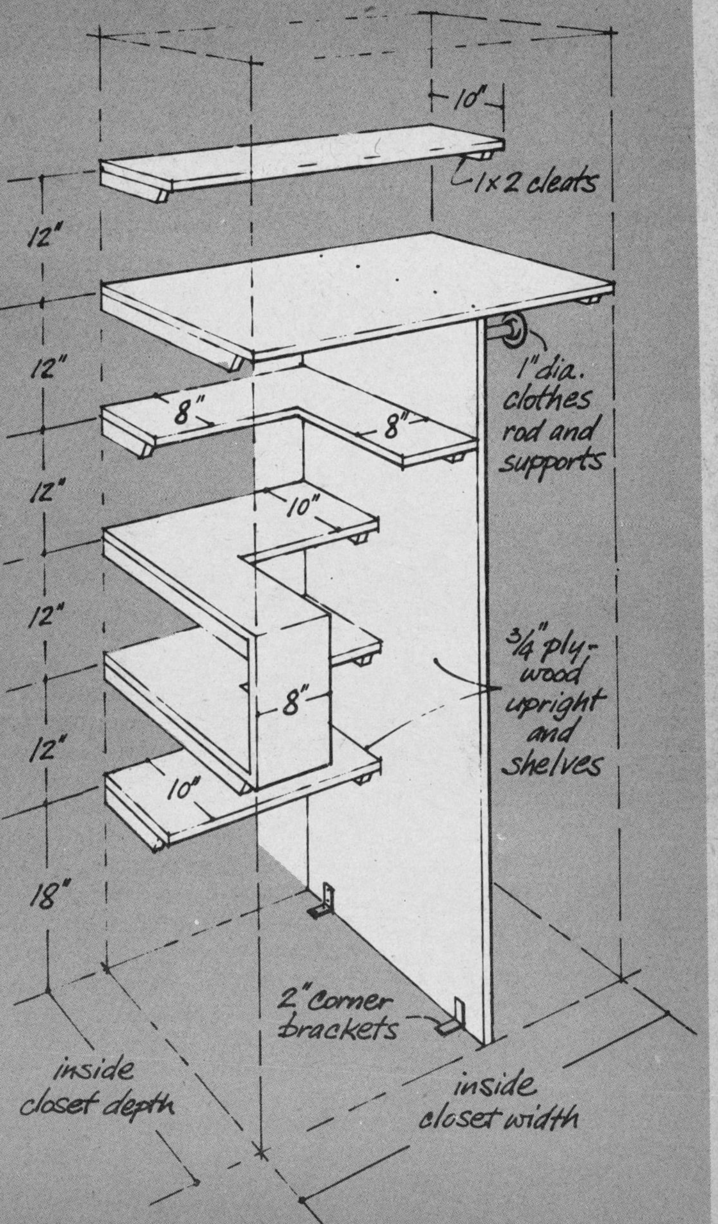
10"
1×2 cleats
12"
12"
8"
8"
1" dia. clothes rod and supports
12"
10"
12"
3/4" plywood upright and shelves
8"
12"
10"
18"
2" corner brackets
inside closet depth
inside closet width

With closet space at a premium in the American home, the pressure is always on to make the best possible use of the storage you have or can contrive. In many homes a spot that can stand improvement is the kitchen closet, where cleaning equipment and supplies are piled willy-nilly, with most of the space going to waste. This closet can be fitted out with shelves that give three or four times as much usable space for supplies and still leave room for hanging aprons and smocks.

The unit shown on the preceding two pages is built entirely of ¾" fir plywood and 1x2 lumber. The sketch shows all dimensions except those that depend on the actual size of your closet. After measuring the closet and incorporating its width and depth into the plan, cut all plywood pieces and shelf cleats. Then nail the cleats to the closet walls and to the plywood upright. Insert the large upper shelf and fasten the upright in place. Add the rest of the shelves and give the entire unit two coats of paint to match your kitchen door.

Ventilation should be provided so fumes from cleaning supplies don't create a fire hazard. If necessary, cut the door at the top and bottom to gain the ½" clearance needed for adequate air circulation.

10 A KITCHEN YOU'LL LOVE TO LIVE IN
- **The Planning**
- **The How-To**

THE PLANNING

When a home is designed for convenience, it follows that "the livin' is easy . . ." because convenience has been, and will continue to be, the key to comfort. Without it, the most luxuriously appointed house is not a real home at all. Convenience in the kitchen looms large in the scheme, for that is where the lady of the house spends many of her waking hours. And, if the kitchen is not tailored to her special needs and wants, her work will be more difficult and will take longer to accomplish.

These factors, and more, are this article's reason for being. The kitchen seen in the photographs on these and the following pages was planned for convenience.

The three photographs on the facing page serve to illustrate a compact and step-saving combination of working units, with no space-wasting features. In the top photo wall and base cabinets and counter continue around a corner. Dishes and glassware have their places in the wall cabinets. Below, a built-in dishwasher breaks the line of base cabinets—but the corner behind the washer is not wasted.

The door shown at a right angle to the washer hides swingout shelves, shown open at bottom right. Pictured at left is the proximity of the washer to the sink, with generous storage space provided for materials used with each, towels, cleansers, etc.

The complete FH kitchen you will see described was executed in such a way as to make duplication easy. If portions of it provide answers to your special problems, any or all sections can be adapted easily to an existing kitchen without the need for complete remodeling. Just take advantage of the sectional construc-

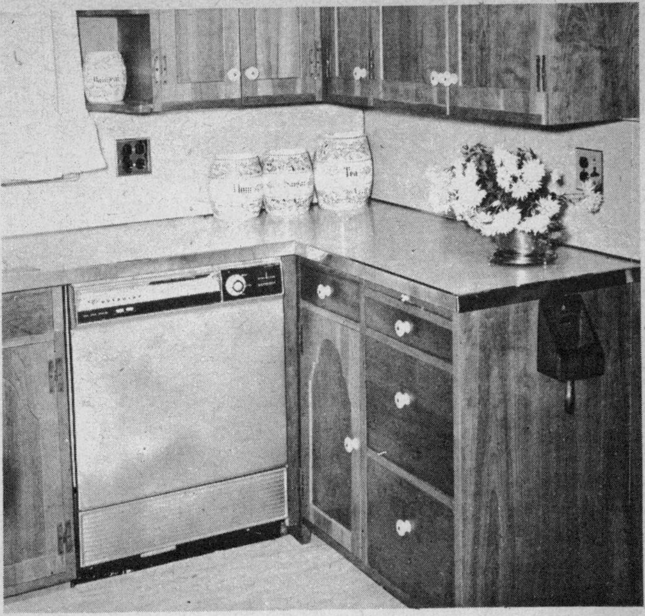
Tea

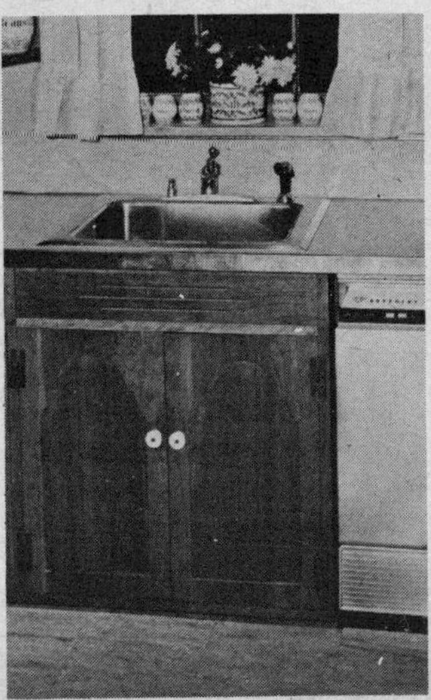

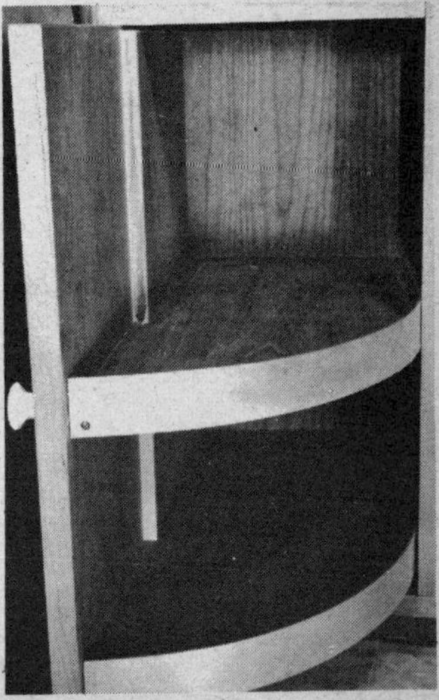

tion that is used throughout.

When you remodel, you have complete control over the three main factors that will determine the usefulness of the room. These are: (1) the amount of cabinet space; (2) the amount of counter space; (3) the location of the appliances in relation to each other and the general plan of the room. Each of these parts contains variables that should be restricted to generally accepted limits. In this category are such items as cabinet depths and counter heights.

It is impossible to have too much storage space in a kitchen, so plan to line all working areas (except those to be occupied by appliances) with base and wall cabinets. If part of the room is to be used for dining, eliminate cabinets from that area to avoid interference with seating and headroom.

Base cabinets should be provided with 3 5/8" toe spaces. Tops should be 36" above the floor, but may be adjusted up or down to fit your own height. However, do not alter this dimension by more than 2" in either direction. Front to back distance (depth) of the base cabinets should be 24" to provide ample storage space and room for building in a dishwasher and a table-top range.

Upper cabinets should be 12" deep. Their height needs special consideration. FH's model kitchen is in an old house, with unusually high ceilings. From the standpoint of appearance, cabinets reaching all the way to the ceiling would have been overbearing. Since sufficient wall space was available to supply more than adequate storage facilities, we decided to foreshorten the cabinets by making soffits to take up the excess space.

Usually shelves should be no higher than 6' above the floor, to be within easy reach. The extra height of this room made it possible to store frequently used material on shelves no higher than the desirable 6' level while still providing *more* space above for dead storage.

Upper cabinets should be hung on the wall so that there is a space of 15 to 17" above the countertop. This wall space should be covered by splashboards that match the countertops.

Provide for at least two cabinet segments that will extend from floor to ceiling. One will be needed for storage of canned goods; the other may be used for cleaning equipment (brooms, brushes, etc.).

Working area (counter space) goes hand in hand with the base cabinets, for the counter also serves as the cabinet top. In some instances, the counter may extend over an area where there is no cabinet. In FH's kitchen, the dishwasher is located where a base cabinet might otherwise be. The counter simply continues over it. Counters may be extended by turning a corner to make a peninsula table at a convenient location. The table adjacent to the range in our plan, detailed later in photos and diagrams, does more than provide additional valuable space, for it is usable as a snack bar, too.

LOCATING THE APPLIANCES

Every kitchen must have a sink, a refrigerator and a range (baking oven may be separate). Ideally, the sides of the triangle they form should add up to less than 22 feet. The distance between the center front of the refrigerator and the center front of the sink should be from 4 to 7', between refrigerator and range, 4 to 9', and between range and sink, 4 to 6'.

The eternal triangle every housewife knows. See text following for optimum dimensions...

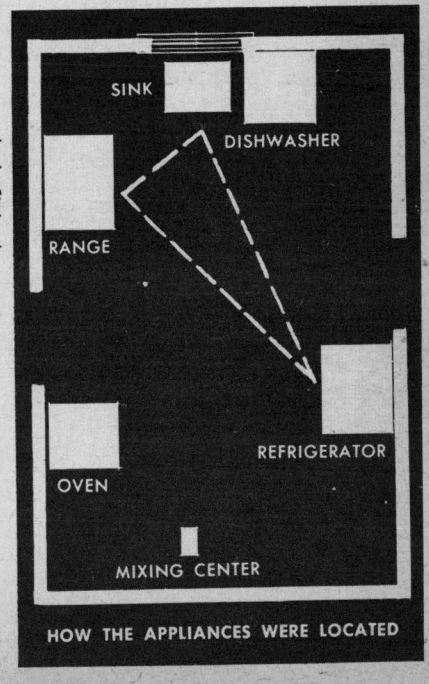

HOW THE APPLIANCES WERE LOCATED

Take care about where you place the range. Keep it far enough away from a window so that curtains can't blow over it, accidentally catching fire; you'll also prevent breezes from extinguishing the burners. Keep it away from a doorway to avoid the danger of hot utensils' being knocked off by traffic into the room.

Traditionally the sink is placed below a window, where the extra light is an advantage. The view will also help to make cleanup time pass more quickly. In the FH kitchen the sink, the built-in range and its adjoining counter and peninsula table, shown in photos on the facing page, are finished in easy-to-maintain stainless steel. Over the range, the hood captures smoke and grease, blowing it outdoors through a hidden duct.

Deciding where the refrigerator is to be may be influenced by the direction in which its door opens. If you plan to purchase a new one for the remodeled room, there is more freedom in locating it.

When plans include a separate baking oven, its location should be decided last. It should have a counter alongside that is capable of resisting the heat of a roasting pan that has just been withdrawn from the oven. Ceramic tile is the best material that can be used here. Having a small area of the counter inlaid with it is recommended. If feasible, you might have one whole section of the counter done in this material. Oven height is determined by counter height. The open oven door should be level with the counter.

PREPARING FOR THE JOB

Deciding on a final plan and following a programmed sequence of operations will do much to make the work flow smoothly. In general terms, plan in the following manner.

The Appliances—you and you alone know what you want. Do you intend to keep the appliances you now have, or replace some or all? If your present kitchen contains only the basic essentials, perhaps you will want to add a dishwasher, a garbage disposal unit or a wall oven. Whatever the decision, it is yours alone—and it is the first step to take. Cabinet sizes and shapes will depend on the appliances' locations and dimensions.

The Floor Plan—lay out the exact plan of the room on graph paper. Draw in the walls, doorways and windows, locating them

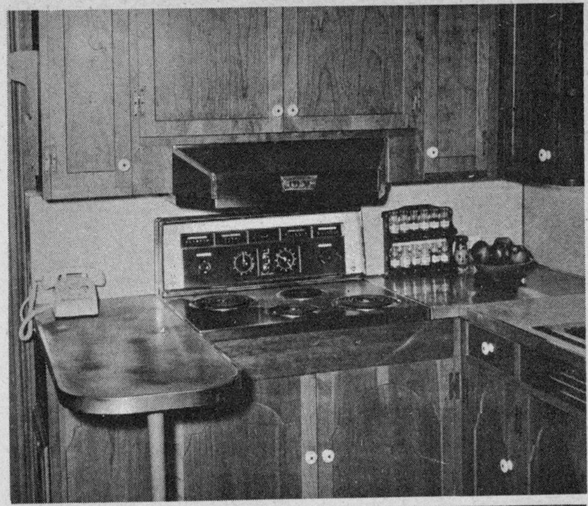

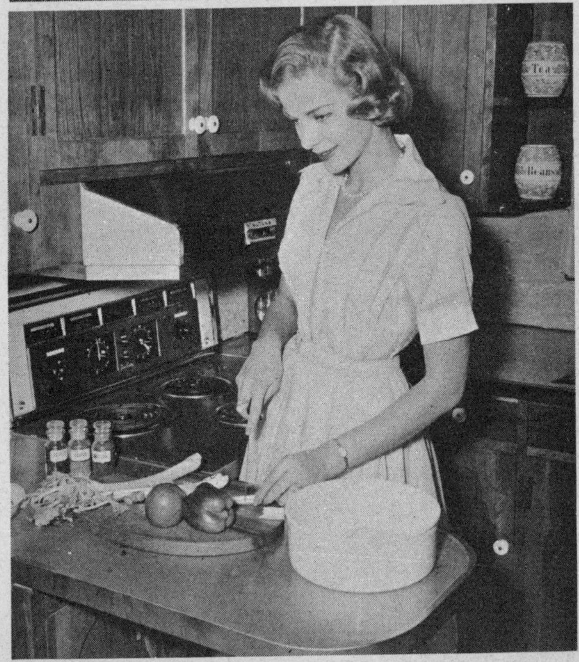
Tea

in their proper positions. Use a scale of at least 1" to the foot; your plan will be easier to draw and more accurate if the scale is even larger. Cut out scaled-down top views of the appliances, using thin cardboard or heavy paper for the "models." Decide their locations by trying them in different positions on the plan, seeing how they fit and measuring the distances between them.

The Utilities—here is where professional help should be expected. Wiring, plumbing and cooking fuel (unless you include an electric stove) must be considered. Good lighting is a must. One overhead fixture will provide an adequate level of general illumination, but a supplementary light source in each work area is equally necessary. There should be a number of convenience outlets for plug-in appliances, such as mixer, toaster, etc. Include at least two double outlets at each work area. Power must be brought to the refrigerator, the dishwasher and all other electrically operated appliances. It is prudent to have the electrician also survey existing wiring, for new lines may have to be drawn from the main service box if heavy use of power is expected. When you know where your sink will be located, you can arrange for a plumber to set in the rough plumbing to which he will later attach the sink and faucets. If you intend to employ gas as the cooking fuel, and if the stove or range will be located away from its present position, contact your gas company and find out what must be done to relocate the fuel lines.

The Cabinet Work—play safe with your future peace of mind and use interior hardware in cabinet drawer construction, as shown above. Metal drawer slides with nylon rollers will keep your cabinets functioning smoothly and provide some leeway with your skills as a carpenter. Also invest in power tools. It is conceivable that a homeowner with a high degree of skill and lots of leisure could remodel a kitchen by using only hand tools, but the work can be done in a fraction of the time and with much more accuracy when power tools are employed. Since the final appearance of the remodeled kitchen will depend mainly on the quality of the carpentry, it is recommended that you purchase a power saw if you don't already have one.

The money to be saved by doing the work yourself will more

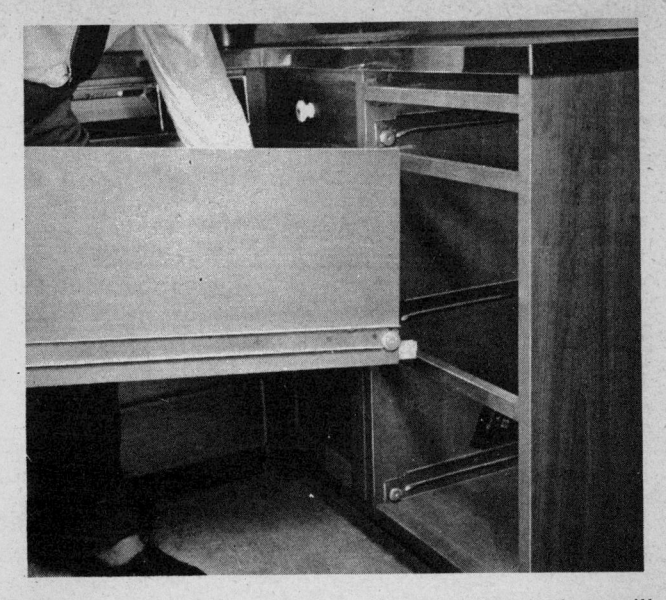

than pay for it. While a table saw will do the job, a beginner will find the radial arm saw easier to use and more versatile. With the proper accessories, it can also do sanding, routing and shaping, operations that will be necessary later. The making of the counters and backsplashes presents another problem. To be properly finished, they should have as few seams as possible, which means that large areas of plastic or stainless steel sheet, laminated to plywood, must be cut into the L-shapes demanded by nearly all kitchen plans. Laminating and forming some unwieldly pieces is best done by a shop. The shop people will also cover the exposed edges with aluminum or stainless steel molding, shaping it around corners wherever necessary. For these reasons, the drawings showing the construction of the various cabinets do not include the tops or the backsplashes. When you start to make the cabinets, allow for the 3/4" thickness of the countertop, taking it into consideration in your work. Remember that counter height should be kept within the limits mentioned previously.

This seems a suitable place to mention the chief raw material used in this project—the plywood. We chose 3/4" lumber-core "Weldwood" cherry plywood for its warmth and richness. Other hardwoods that can be processed to fine "furniture" finishes are also available. Regardless of which you use, obtain the lumber-core variety. Its cut edges are better—holes are few and far between. Because of this, the edges are easier to finish with flexible wood tape. Screws driven into it get a better grip. At your local lumber yard, compare samples of this type with the ordinary variety of plywood. You'll see and understand the difference at once. Counters and backsplash surfaces to be covered with stainless steel or plastic laminates can be made or lower-priced plywood or flakeboard.

To Get Started—if you can arrange for a place where meals can be prepared while work progresses, you will have solved a major problem. An easy way out is available to those fortunate families whose homes have a "spare" kitchen, perhaps adjoining the basement recreation room. If you can't do either of these, two choices still remain. The most practical is to leave the sink and old appliances connected as long as possible, working around them; the other is to set up temporary facilities in another room. No matter what the situation or your solution, there will be temporary inconvenience and dislocation until the job is done. Face it squarely.

Removing the old cabinets and fixtures is the first step. Work with care, preserving wall surfaces as much as possible. A small wrecking bar is a help in this job. If several layers of wallpaper have accumulated throughout the years, this is the time to remove them. A steamer rented from your nearest paint-and-paper dealer will do the job quickly. Patch all cracks and holes in the plaster and prime the repaired areas with shellac or glue size, if new wallpaper is to be hung.

Get a good start by building and installing the upper cabinets first. Since appliances and sink are floor-based, much can be accomplished this way without depriving yourself entirely of the use of the kitchen. With these done, work can begin on the lower cabinets. It's best to build them in the workshop, installing them one by one until all are in place. Make sure that individual units assembled this way are small enough to pass through the doorways between shop and kitchen, or you may find yourself a cousin to the well-known unfortunate who built a big boat in his basement...

On the following pages, you'll find the instructions and detailed drawings for building the units seen in the accompanying photographs. It's a big project, so make sure that you plan carefully, making the necessary adaptations to fit your own kitchen and your own tastes. Then take your time, and build well!

THE HOW-TO

The layouts of the wall and base cabinets of the FH kitchen are shown in the diagrams on this and the facing pages. Wall cabinets are shown below, base cabinets (and appliances) directly opposite. Three segments—J, F and E—continuous from floor to ceiling, appear in both. The diagrams indicate how the individual cabinets fit together to line the room.

Each unit is identified by a letter that denotes the sketch illustrating its construction. For example, the unit

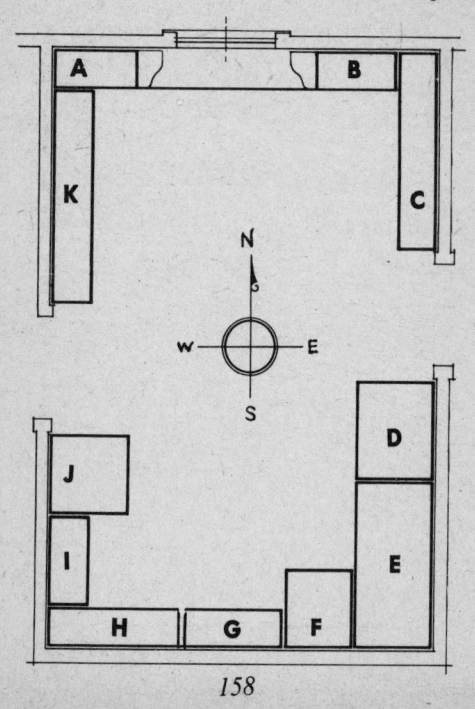

158

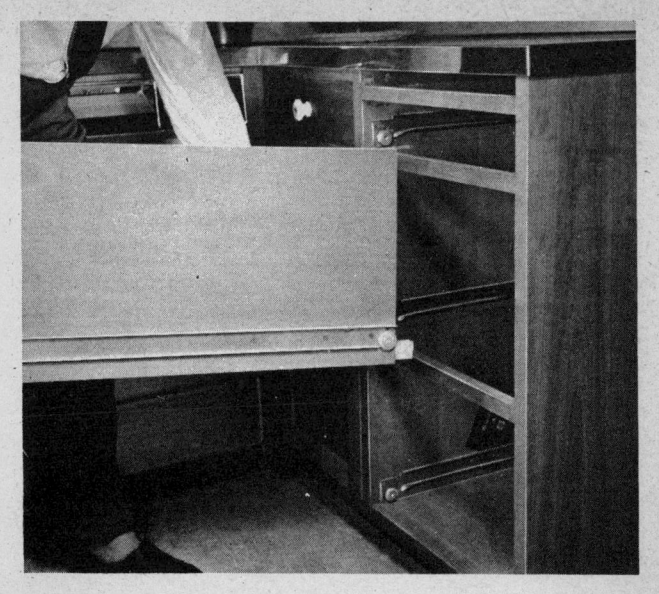

than pay for it. While a table saw will do the job, a beginner will find the radial arm saw easier to use and more versatile. With the proper accessories, it can also do sanding, routing and shaping, operations that will be necessary later. The making of the counters and backsplashes presents another problem. To be properly finished, they should have as few seams as possible, which means that large areas of plastic or stainless steel sheet, laminated to plywood, must be cut into the L-shapes demanded by nearly all kitchen plans. Laminating and forming some unwieldly pieces is best done by a shop. The shop people will also cover the exposed edges with aluminum or stainless steel molding, shaping it around corners wherever necessary. For these reasons, the drawings showing the construction of the various cabinets do not include the tops or the backsplashes. When you start to make the cabinets, allow for the 3/4" thickness of the countertop, taking it into consideration in your work. Remember that counter height should be kept within the limits mentioned previously.

This seems a suitable place to mention the chief raw material used in this project—the plywood. We chose 3/4" lumber-core "Weldwood" cherry plywood for its warmth and richness. Other hardwoods that can be processed to fine "furniture" finishes are also available. Regardless of which you use, obtain the lumber-core variety. Its cut edges are better—holes are few and far between. Because of this, the edges are easier to finish with flexible wood tape. Screws driven into it get a better grip. At your local lumber yard, compare samples of this type with the ordinary variety of plywood. You'll see and understand the difference at once. Counters and backsplash surfaces to be covered with stainless steel or plastic laminates can be made or lower-priced plywood or flakeboard.

To Get Started—if you can arrange for a place where meals can be prepared while work progresses, you will have solved a major problem. An easy way out is available to those fortunate families whose homes have a "spare" kitchen, perhaps adjoining the basement recreation room. If you can't do either of these, two choices still remain. The most practical is to leave the sink and old appliances connected as long as possible, working around them; the other is to set up temporary facilities in another room. No matter what the situation or your solution, there will be temporary inconvenience and dislocation until the job is done. Face it squarely.

Removing the old cabinets and fixtures is the first step. Work with care, preserving wall surfaces as much as possible. A small wrecking bar is a help in this job. If several layers of wallpaper have accumulated throughout the years, this is the time to remove them. A steamer rented from your nearest paint-and-paper dealer will do the job quickly. Patch all cracks and holes in the plaster and prime the repaired areas with shellac or glue size, if new wallpaper is to be hung.

Get a good start by building and installing the upper cabinets first. Since appliances and sink are floor-based, much can be accomplished this way without depriving yourself entirely of the use of the kitchen. With these done, work can begin on the lower marked "A" at the left, appears in detail in Sketch A, later on in this article.

Now for some general information about the "how-to" of this story. *Read it carefully and mark this page for future reference—you may want to come back to it as the work progresses.*

It isn't likely that your kitchen is the same size as FH's. Since our cabinets were, of necessity, made to fit our room, it should be understood that the dimensions given here are meant to serve only as guides rather than rigid specifications. Heights and depths should be maintained, as specified; widths will have to be adjusted to fit your room.

To avoid constant repetition, some frequently used construction steps are given here:

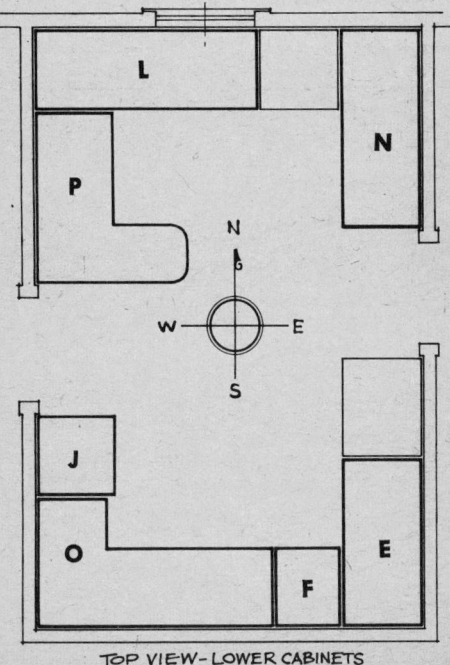

TOP VIEW—LOWER CABINETS

1) Use glue and countersunk flathead screws at all joints.

2) Fill holes over recessed screwheads with wood putty and sand smooth when dry.

3) Finish all exposed plywood edges by gluing matching wood tape over them.

4) Interior cabinet hardware (adjustable shelf brackets, magnetic catches, etc.) should be affixed after a cabinet is built, but before it is hung.

5) Wall cabinets may be supported on cleats fastened to studs. Screws driven into the wall studs through the backs of the cabinets will hold them firmly.

6) Base cabinets need anchoring only through the backs. Two screws in each section are driven into wall studs.

7) Instructions for making the doors to fit every cabinet will appear in the final section of this article.

We mentioned earlier that the upper shelves of the wall cabinets should be no higher than 6' from the floor for easy access. If your kitchen has a high ceiling you will need soffits to close the gap between cabinet tops and ceiling.

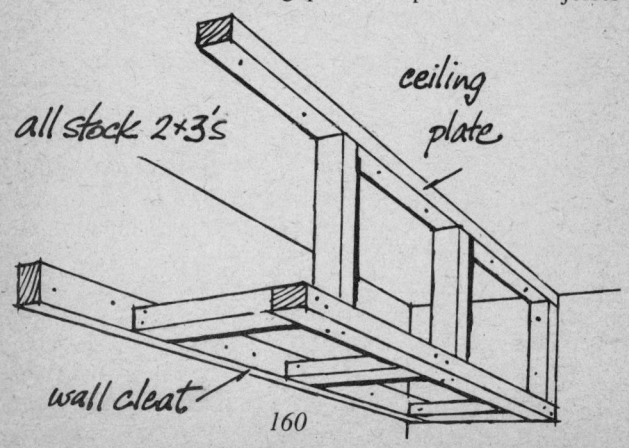

Soffits are framed from 2x3's in the manner shown in the sketch below. A ceiling plate is spiked to the joists above and the wall cleat is spiked to the studs. The short 2x3's between the main members are toe-nailed in place. Afterward, the face of the soffit is covered with wallboard or any convenient sheet material. When the cabinets are hung, gaps remaining between the bottom of the soffit and the tops of the cabinets will be hidden by a cove molding that is last to be affixed.

So much for the basics. We're now ready to go into details of the individual cabinet construction.

A and B—The Window Wall Cabinets—see the layout on page 158. The finished cabinet is shown in the photograph above and the construction diagram on the following page.

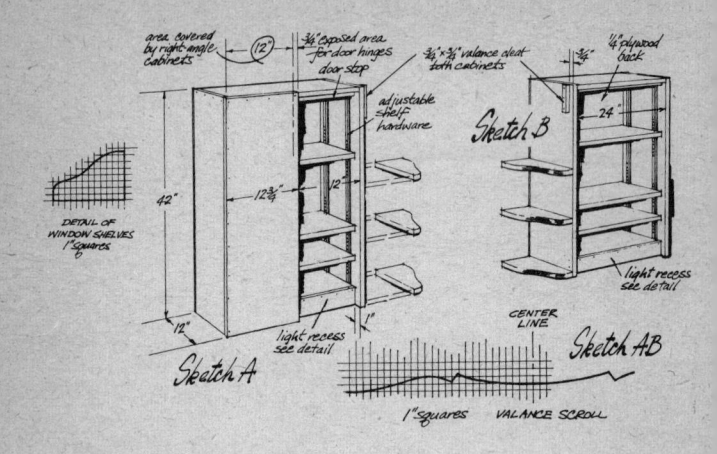

When the kitchen window is located near the center of the wall, the design of the cabinets along that wall should be as symmetrical as practical. Here, the cabinets adjoining each side of the window are similar to each other and are unified by the wood valance that joins them at the top. (See Sketch AB for valance pattern.) The left and right side cabinets (Sketches A and B respectively) are made independently of each other. Notice that one end of Cabinet A will be out of sight when the cabinet that hangs on the wall at its left is positioned. When cabinets reach all the way into the corners, as they do here, no space is wasted.

At the bottoms of both Cabinet A and B, space is provided for recessing fluorescent light fixtures to provide illumination for the work surfaces below. A drawing showing the construction in detail is included with Sketch C on page 165.

There are three small display shelves on the window side of each cabinet. These are cut from 3/4" stock and affixed with glue and finishing nails driven through the cabinet sides.

The West Wall Cabinet—check unit K in the appliance-placement diagram on page 164 and you will note that a place must be made in the cabinet (photos and Sketch K are shown above and on the facing page) over the range for the ventilating hood and its duct.

Care must be taken in this assembly to avoid difficulty when installing the hood and duct. Before starting, check the cabinet's dimensions against those of the hood and duct you intend to use. Make sure they will fit. Do not enclose the soffit above this area until the very end. Build the cabinet, completing it except for the framing that will close in the hood, the intermediate center shelf and the 14" board in front of the duct. Install the cabinet on the wall.

Next fasten the hood to the underside with the hardware furnished and slide the duct into place from above. Install as much additional duct as needed, to reach the

Sketch K

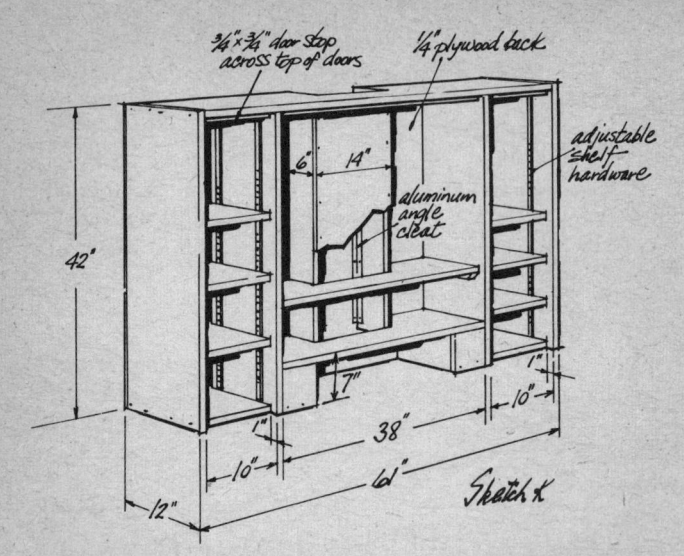

- ¾" × ¾" door stop across top of doors
- ¼" plywood back
- adjustable shelf hardware
- aluminum angle cleat
- 42"
- 6"
- 14"
- 7"
- 1"
- 10"
- 38"
- 10"
- 1"
- 61"
- 12"

exterior wall. Nail the 14" duct cover in place, cutting it in two if necessary. Last, install the large intermediate shelf that stretches the width of the cabinet. It should be pointed out that this shelf is the only one in the kitchen that was not made adjustable; it was preferable to fasten it permanently in place on cleats, because of the large oblong opening that must be cut in it to permit passage of the duct. As the final step here, cover the soffit, once the ductwork is complete.

The final result is shown in the lower photo on the preceding page.

The East Wall Cabinet—refer to the kitchen layout diagram on page 158 and photo and construction diagrams below and on the next page—extends into the northeast corner of the room, where it fits between window cabinet B and the east wall. As seen in Sketch C (below), it is a single cabinet divided by a vertical board, which makes it seem two separate units.

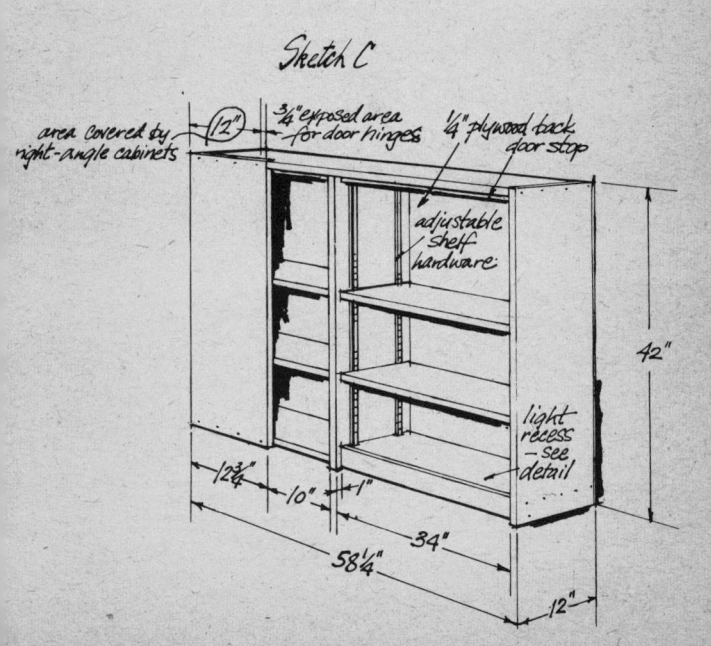

Sketch C

- area covered by right-angle cabinets
- (12")
- 3/4" exposed area for door hinges
- 1/4" plywood back door stop
- adjustable shelf hardware
- light recess—see detail
- 12 3/4"
- 10"
- 1"
- 34"
- 58 1/4"
- 42"
- 12"

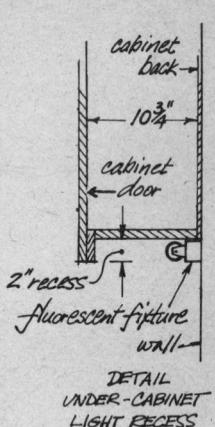

cabinet back
← 10¾" →
cabinet door
2" recess
fluorescent fixture
wall

DETAIL
UNDER-CABINET
LIGHT RECESS

A recess on its bottom provides a place for the fixture that will light the work surface beneath—see diagram at right above.

When you undertake a major remodeling project such as is shown on these pages, you should proceed in stages, just as it is being presented. On the following pages we complete the northern end of the room—base cabinets and counters, with built-in appliances—and get started on the other end of the job—the mixing center and the cabinets above it.

The Window Wall Base cabinet (refer to L in base cabinet layout on page 159 and construction diagram—Sketch L—on the page 167) makes provision in the FH kitchen for both dishwasher and the sink and is designed to provide adequate storage for materials and accessories used with both installations.

The exact dimensions of base cabinet L depend on two variables—the amount of space that is required for the dishwasher you've selected, and the length of the wall. It

SKETCH L

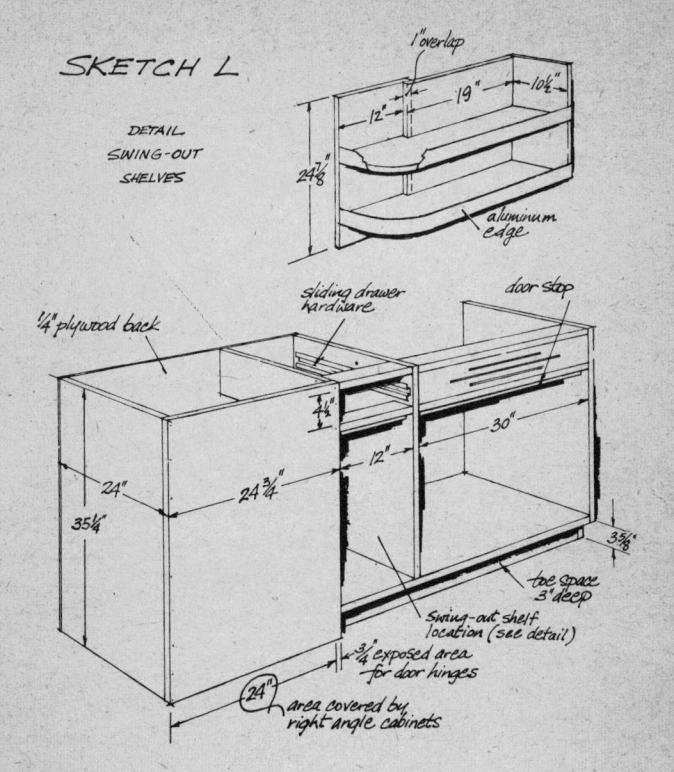

DETAIL SWING-OUT SHELVES

is best to allow at least 2" more than the actual requirements for the dishwasher to permit easier access to the machine for adjustment or repair. The extra space may be concealed by attaching a vertical cleat of appropriate width to the side of one of the cabinets which adjoin the opening. Fasten the cleats with screws only, to permit easy removal when necessary. Upper photo on the following page shows the cleat at right.

Putting the cabinet together is mainly a matter of cutting the pieces to size, following the details seen in the accompanying sketch. The back of the 30" wide section

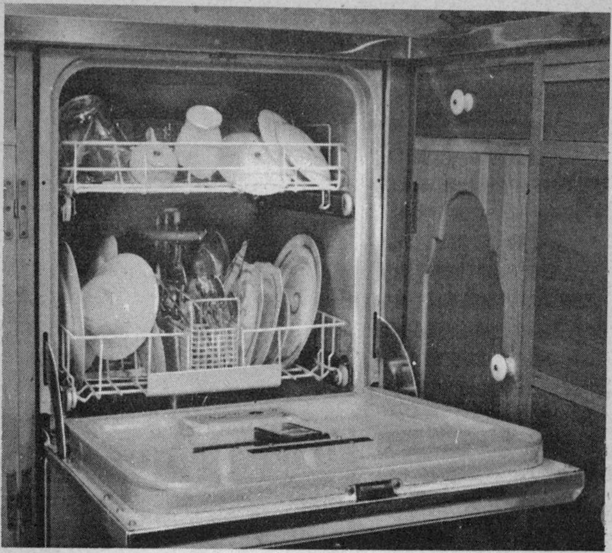

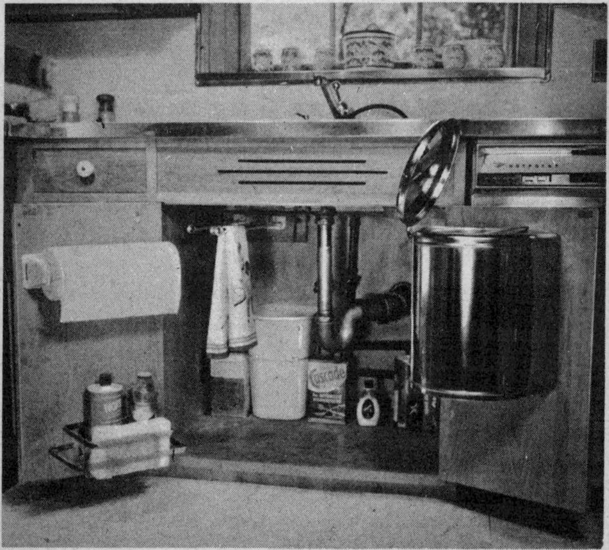

is left open so that plumbing can be connected to the sink that will be installed in the counter. See the lower photo on the preceding page and note the use of doors and under-the-sink space for supplies, towels, concealed garbage can.

Other parts of the cabinet are backed with 1/4" plywood. We used cherry plywood here to make the insides of the cabinet match exteriors. But, if economy is your goal, pine plywood stained to match will cost less.

From the diagram showing the floor plan of the kitchen, page 159, it will be observed that all four corners of the room are occupied by cabinets; no space is wasted. To provide access to these special areas, swing-out shelves have been fitted to the corner cabinets. The shelves are attached to the door and move outward when it is opened. In the illustration above, swing-out shelves handy to the area are used to store cooking utensils.

Construction of these shelves is shown in the detail sketch at the top of page 183. The rounded edge of the shelves is cut with a sabre saw on the arc of a circle with a radius of 12", measured on the piece that forms the door. The shelves are attached to concealed 3/4x3/4" cleats, which are glued and screwed to the door. Strip aluminum, 2" wide, obtainable at most hardware stores, is bent around the curve and attached to the edges with screws. The strip prevents any objects stored on the shelves from slipping off.

When the swinging shelves are completed, they are attached to the cabinet proper with antique style H-hinges, which are used throughout. Magnet catches, top and bottom, will hold the door firmly closed. Decorative wood trim may be applied last. Detailed instructions for applying the trim will be found in a later section.

The space above the swing-out shelves is filled with a drawer, mounted on metal slides to assure easy operation. Typical drawer construction is shown in the diagram on page 173.

The Base Cabinet on the West Wall is the next step in our remodeling program.

Three functions are fulfilled by this single component of FH's kitchen (P, in diagram on page 159). It provides a base for the range with ample space below for storage of cooking utensils. One end of the cabinet encloses a radiator—you may want to modify the facing shown in the photo to suit your choice of heating unit.

Above this area, a peninsula table extends toward the center of the room. It may be used as a snack bar, or as additional work space.

The construction diagram is shown on the facing page.

To adopt this cabinet to your own needs, you will first need to know the exact space requirements of the range of your choice. This information may be obtained from the manufacturer's literature, or from your appliance dealer.

Be absolutely certain of the dimensions before proceed-

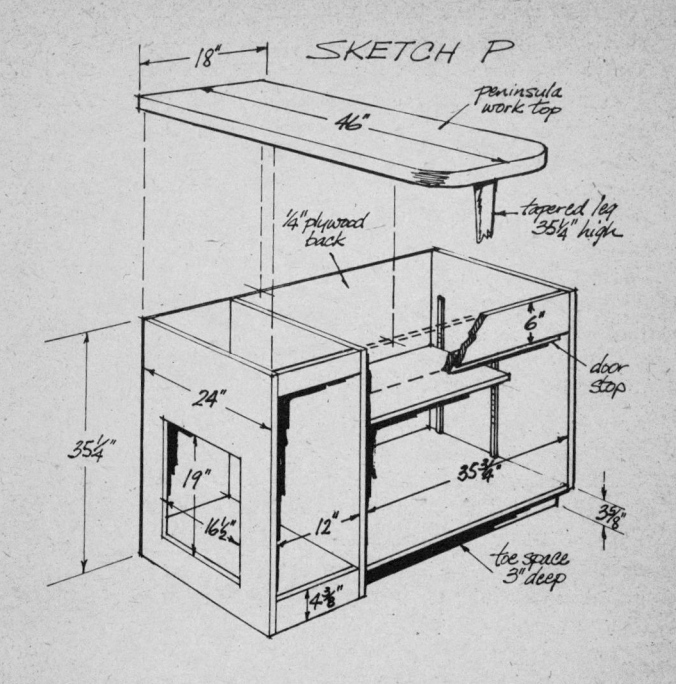

SKETCH P — peninsula work top, 18″, 46″, ¼″ plywood back, tapered leg 35¼″ high, 6″, door stop, 24″, 19″, 16½″, 35¼″, 12″, 35¾″, 3⅞″, 4⅜″, toe space 3″ deep

ing—if possible, measure the actual unit you intend to purchase at your dealer's. Diagrams are not always accurate in these times of sudden model changes.

The "radiator" end of the cabinet may also need adjustment, unless the rather rare and specialized heater we used is to be installed in it. The FH radiator uses water, hot in the winter, cold in the summer. A blower fan is part of the unit and circulates the treated air over a surprisingly large area.

The cabinet floor is optional; when an ordinary hot-water or steam radiator is to be enclosed it may be more convenient to eliminate the floor. The size of the opening into which the radiator fits may also change, depending on the type of heater used. For the conventional radiator

171

you may wish to make the opening larger, for better heat circulation, and cover it with a piece of perforated aluminum, cut to fit.

If you are having the countertops made by a professional, the peninsula table top should be part of his job since its covering material should match that used for the adjacent counter. The table—your job—is fastened to the cabinet by cleats attached to its underside, through which screws are driven into the sides of the cabinet.

The access door at the front of the radiator section may be held in place by magnetic catches, as it is seldom removed, or it can be attached with hinges in the usual manner. A pattern for cutting the decorative overlay on the door appears in a later section.

The Base Cabinet on the East Wall is shown completed on the following page—the construction diagram (Sketch N) below.

This segment of the kitchen cabinetry (refer to N, diagram on page 159), is the piece that completes the northern end of the room. Storage is the basic function of the unit—but the storage is specialized. One compartment is occupied by drawers for table silverware and baked goods, with a convenient sliding cutting-board above. Bread drawers are fitted with sheet metal bread boxes that keep breads and cakes fresh (see photo on following page).

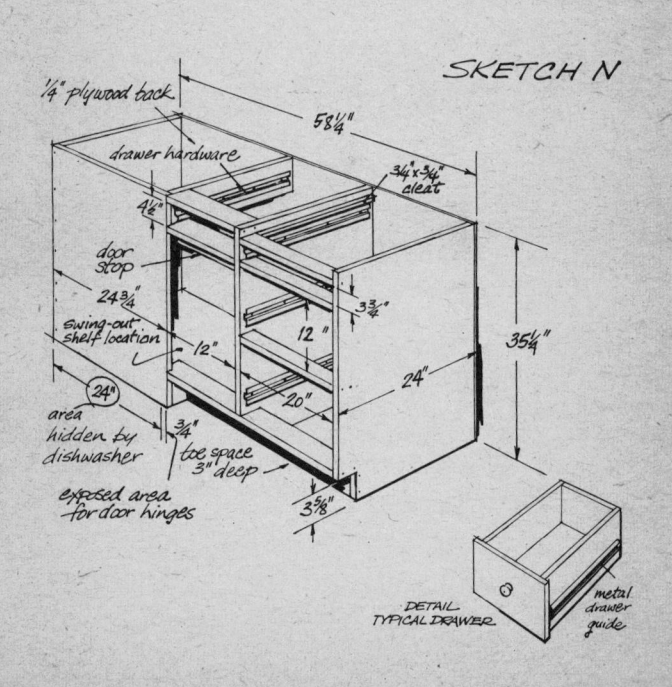

SKETCH N

- ¼" plywood back
- drawer hardware
- 58¼"
- ¾" x ¾" cleat
- 4½"
- door stop
- 24¾"
- swing-out shelf location
- 12"
- 3¾"
- 12"
- 35¼"
- 24"
- 20"
- 24"
- area hidden by dishwasher
- ¾"
- toe space 3" deep
- exposed area for door hinges
- 3⅝"

DETAIL TYPICAL DRAWER
metal drawer guide

All drawers operate smoothly on metal slides that can't be affected by dampness, making sticking drawers a thing of the past. The cutting-board is not slide-mounted because of its 3/4" thickness. It rests on 3/4x 3/4" cleats fastened to the uprights.

The section to the left is topped by a utility drawer, while underneath are swing-out shelves—exact duplicates of those fitted to base cabinets L. (Refer to Sketch L, page 167, for construction details.) The blind face of the cabinet, adjacent to the swing-out shelf door, becomes the right side of the dishwasher enclosure when the cabinet is positioned.

Cut and assemble all the parts, following the sketch carefully. Install drawer slides and cabinet hardware. Position and attach the swing-out shelves with a pair of H-hinges.

Detail drawing of a typical drawer made from 3/4" stock is included. This type of construction may be followed throughout the room, in all cabinets where drawers are specified.

Photo above shows the south end of our kitchen. If you've reached this point, you've come a long way in your kitchen remodeling project.

By now you're practically a master cabinetmaker. The final phases of the job, described on the following pages, should no longer present problems to you.

The Floor-to-ceiling Cabinets are your next step.

Three of the cabinets in FH's kitchen extend the entire distance from floor to ceiling. To be more accurate in this description, they actually fit between the underside of the soffit and the floor. The height of each of these is indicated on the sketches (see Sketches E, J and F on the following pages) as 96", but you should plan them to be 1/4" shorter than the actual space you have to fill. By making the cabinets a little shorter than the space, they can be moved into position easily. The gap, small as it is, will be hidden when molding is applied later at the soffit line.

In keeping with the theme of utilizing every available space, cabinet E (see Sketch E on the facing page) extends into the southeast corner of the room. It is large enough to be called a "walk-in" if the shelves fitted to it are restricted to a width of 10" or less. The shelves are placed along the back (east wall) and one side (south wall), in an L-shape. The smaller, upper portion of the cabinet is used for utility storage, while the large lower part with its separate door and shallow shelves, is designed for storing quantities of canned goods and groceries.

The next member of the trio—Cabinet J—is the most specialized. It provides a place for the wall oven. The dimensions of the oven opening, as shown in the sketch on page 00, must be followed exactly if this is the oven you plan to buy. Otherwise, changes will be necessary.

Many wall ovens, including this one, need only to be inserted in a frame, for they are sold as a "package," complete with integral thermal insulation. The space in the cabinet not needed for the oven is put to good use. Over the oven, a swing-out door reveals a compartment for tray storage. Above that, utility space is fitted with an

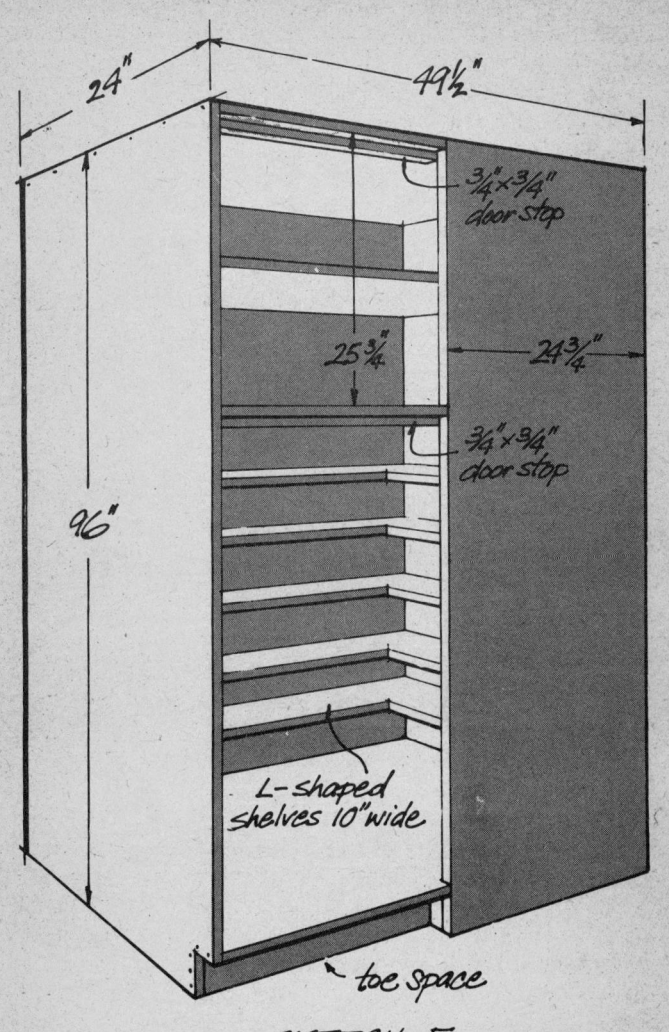

SKETCH E

adjustable shelf. Under the oven, a deep drawer suitable for larger utensils, baking pans and other bulky pieces completes the unit.

After the unit is assembled, your electrician will have to install the wiring necessary for the oven—or, if gas is to be the fuel, openings in the back of Cabinet J will have to be made for the wires or pipes. After this has

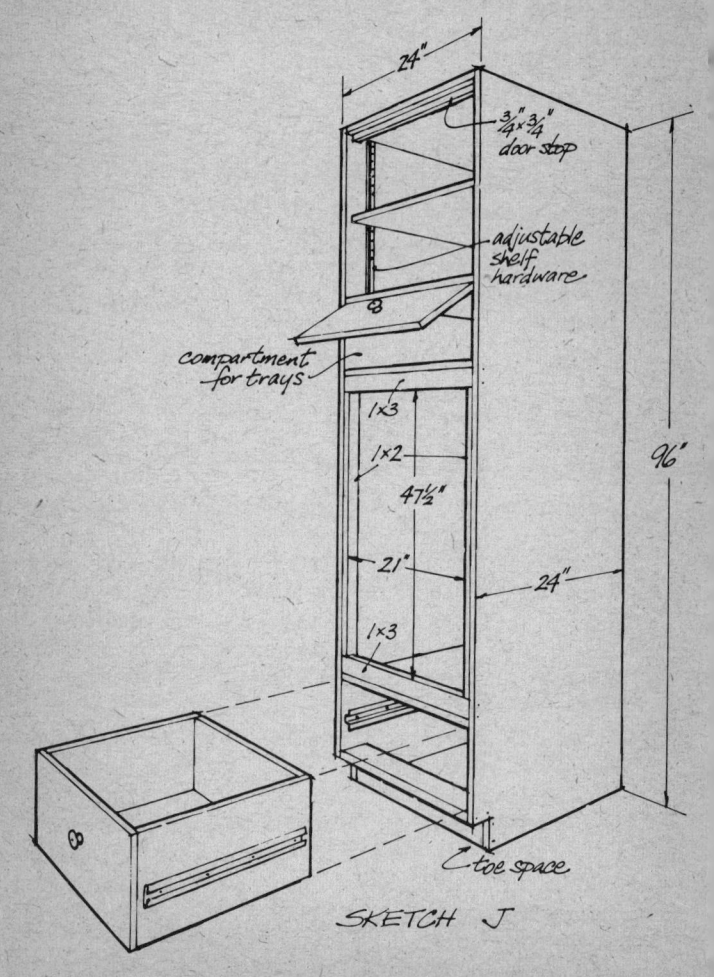

SKETCH J

SKETCH F

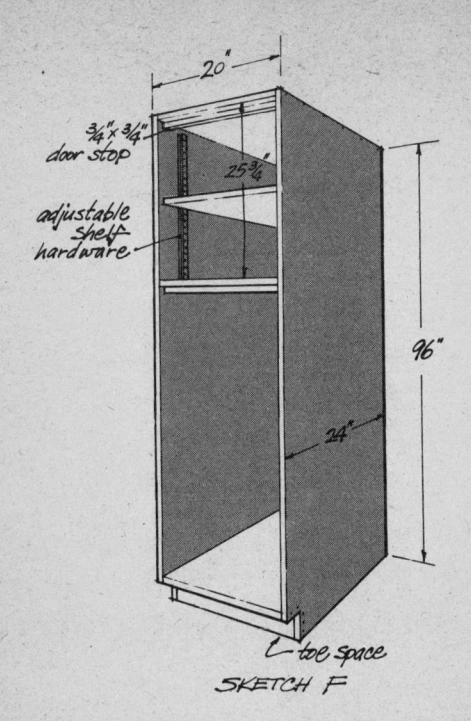

been done, and the utility supply lines have been drawn to the proper location by the contractor, the cabinet may be positioned.

Cabinet F, like E, is divided into two parts. The lower part is planned for use as a broom closet; there is ample space to store brushes, mops, brooms and an assortment of house cleaning supplies. The upper part can be used for similar materials or for general storage.

The construction diagram is shown above.

The South End Wall Cabinet Assembly is the next and all but the final step in our remodeling.

Of the wall cabinets still remaining to be built, three (D, H and I; see sketches on the next two pages) are simply boxes of varying dimensions. The fourth—G, shown with Sketch H on page 181—is only part of a box. One

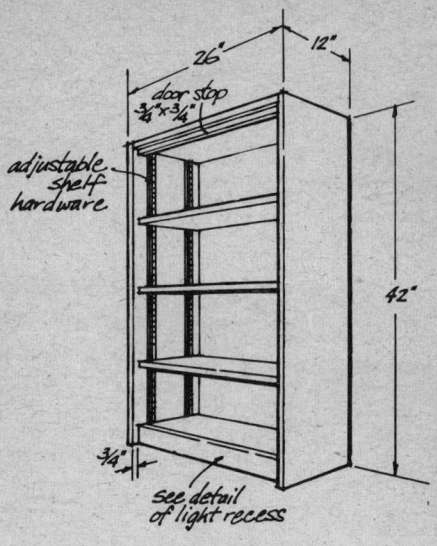

SKETCH I

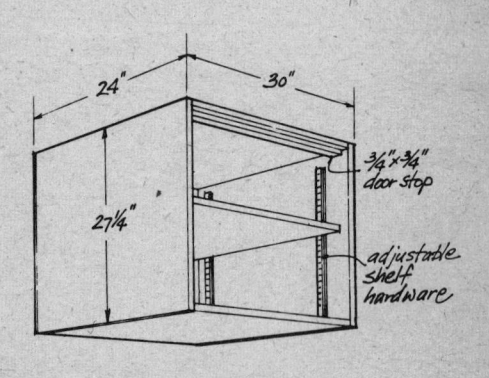

SKETCH D

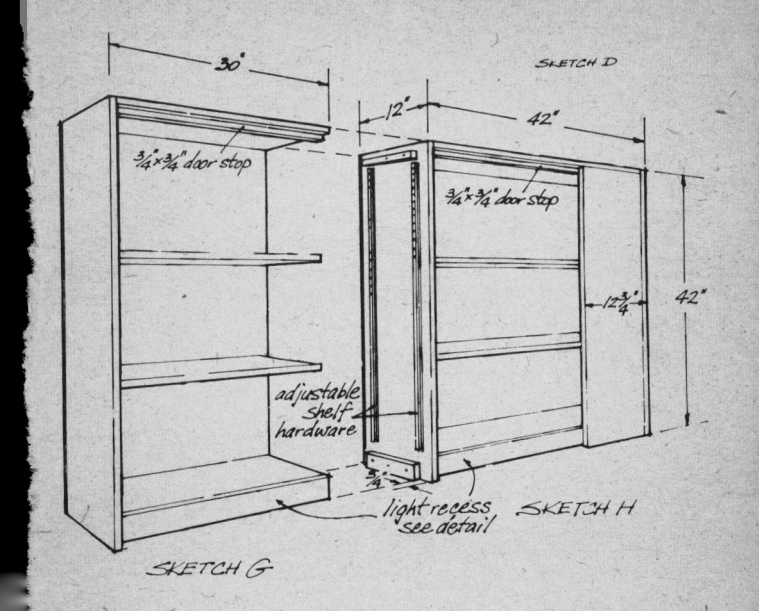

side of Cabinet H also serves as the end of G when both are hung on the wall. The joint is made by attaching cleats to the exterior surface of the left side of H; the open right end of G then fits over the cleats and the pieces are permanently joined with screws and glue.

The dimensions of Cabinet D, which occupies the space above the refrigerator, are controlled by the refrigerator's size. Measure the distance between the top of the refrigerator and the bottom of the soffit. Plan to make D about 3" less than this dimension, to allow air circulation around and above the refrigerator. The width of D, given as 30" in the sketch, should also be adjusted to match the width of the refrigerator, if different from this figure.

Cabinet I requires no special consideration other than existing wall space. Its depth and height match other cabinets in the room.

A detail drawing of the light recess, as indicated on Sketches G, H and I, may be found on page 166.

The Corner Base Cabinet—the entire southern end of the room contains only one of the type previously described as a "base cabinet." The sketch showing this unit (sketch O, facing page) details its construction.

A prominent feature here is the large, two-tiered revolving shelf unit—shown in action in the two photos above—which differs substantially from the previously illustrated type used in the other corners of the room. This one is built around a specific type of hardware, rather than simply hanging by its hinges, like the others. The doors are fastened together in an L-shape and, when closed, hide the revolving shelves completely, as at above left. Photo at right shows the special revolving hardware inside.

The sketch illustrates the way the cabinet is built. The construction is straightforward, the bottom being cut from one sheet of plywood into an L-shape. Stretchers hold the uprights and back together rigidly.

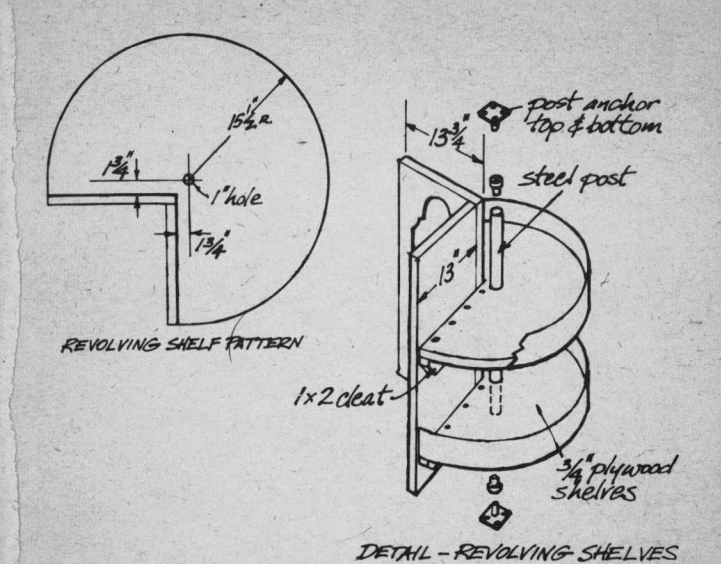

REVOLVING SHELF PATTERN

- $15\frac{1}{2}"$ R
- $1\frac{3}{4}"$
- 1" hole
- $1\frac{3}{4}"$

DETAIL – REVOLVING SHELVES

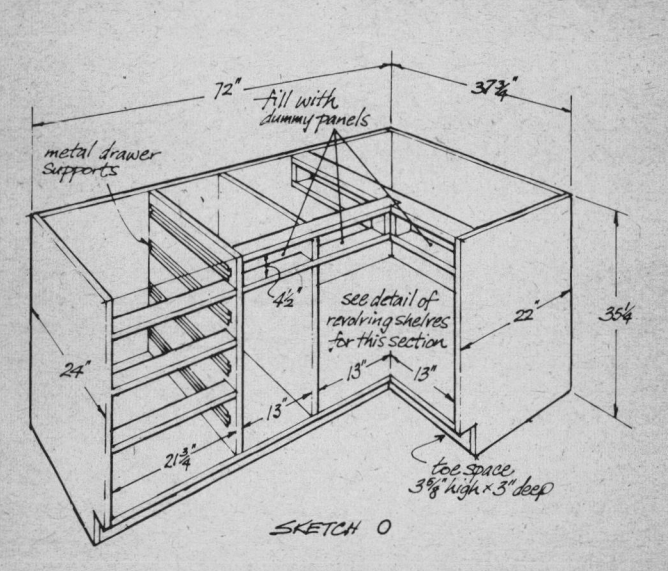

- post anchor top & bottom
- $13\frac{3}{4}"$
- steel post
- 13"
- 1 x 2 cleat
- $\frac{3}{4}"$ plywood shelves

SKETCH O

- 72"
- fill with dummy panels
- $37\frac{3}{4}"$
- metal drawer supports
- $4\frac{1}{2}"$
- see detail of revolving shelves for this section
- 22"
- $35\frac{1}{4}"$
- 24"
- 13"   13"
- $21\frac{3}{4}"$
- toe space, $3\frac{5}{8}"$ high x 3" deep

The revolving shelf is fitted to the cabinet after the basic framework is made. Its front consists of two door panels screwed and glued together at right angles. Discs with a radius of 15 ½" from which a wedge has been cut (detailed on next page) are slipped over the steep post and screwed to cleats on the doors. Strips of aluminum, fastened to the rims of the discs, provide a retaining wall for the stored material when the shelves are in use.

The small corner spaces that would normally be used for drawers are covered with dummy panels instead because there is no room for opposing drawers to open in such a location. The third panel to the left of the corner also substitutes for a drawer, the space being occupied by the mechanism of the food mixing center built into the countertop later. If the mixing center is eliminated, a drawer can actually be made for this place instead.

The Cabinet Doors provide much of the charm of the FH kitchen. Their graceful pattern and the warm shade and subdued grain of the cherry veneer enhance the appearance of the entire room.

Generally, the skill and patience of the builder set the limit on the scope of the cabinet work he can do using hand tools alone. But, with modern power tools in his hands, even the novice can duplicate the results attained by the experienced professional.

The power tool that makes it possible in this instance is the router. This basically simple device with its ultra-high speed cutter, enables you to achieve a professional finish on wood edges, shaping them cleanly in any desired design. If you don't own a router, one can be rented for a few dollars.

The doors are made by cutting and shaping pieces of ¼" cherry plywood rectangles, like a frame. The combination of the two layers makes the finished door. In its completed state, the thickness of the door is 1" at the edges, where the "frame" is, but only 3/4" in the center area. Each "frame" actually consists of four pieces: three rectangles (the sides and bottom) and one curved piece (the top).

Pattern #1—10"

Pattern #2—12"

Pattern #3—13"

PATTERN NO.	FOR CABINET	DOORS NEEDED
1 (10")	C	1
	K	2
2 (12")	A	1
	B	2
	J	2
	L	1
	N	1
	P	1
3 (13")	I	2
	O	3
4 (14¼")	H	2
5 (14⅝")	G	2
6 (15")	D	2
	L	2
7 (17")	C	2
8 (17⅞")	P	2
9 (18½")	F	2
10 (19")	K	2
11 (24")	E	2

Pattern #4—14¼"

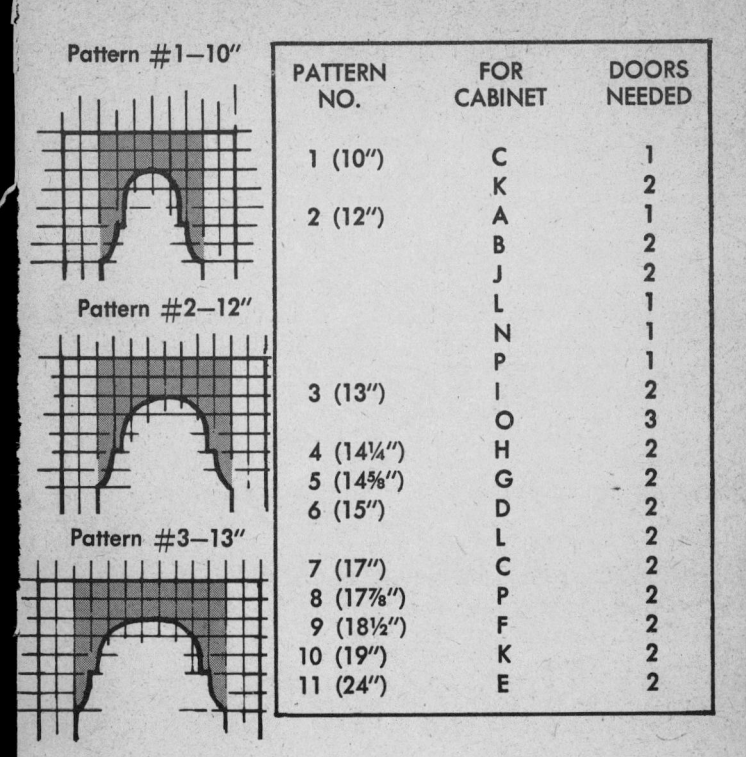

Pattern #5—14⅝"

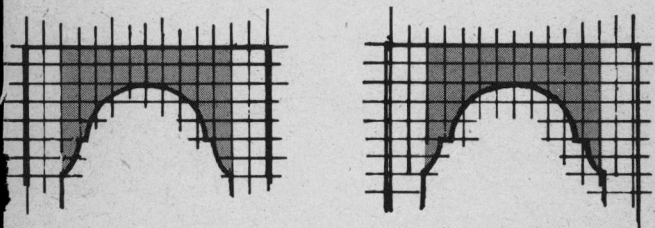

The sketches above and on the next page give the pattern details for the doors. Each square represents 1x1". To begin, cut rectangles from 3/4" stock to the door sizes needed—and as many of each as needed (see table above). Next, lay out from pattern of the curved piece on ¼"

Pattern #6—15"

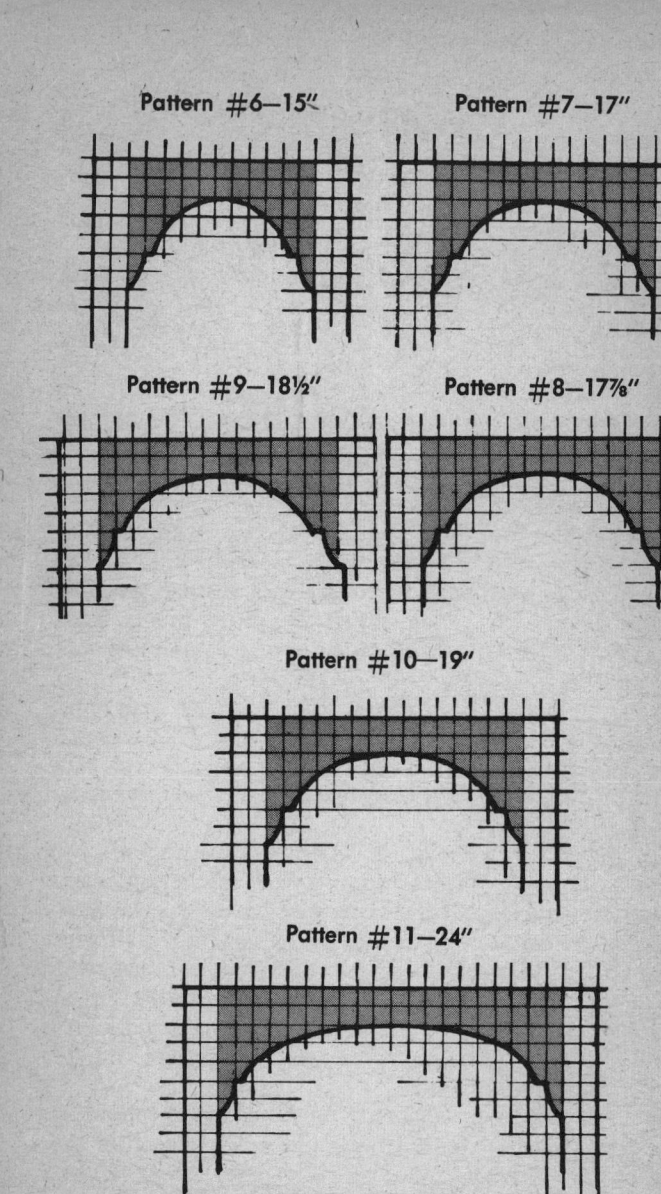

Pattern #7—17"

Pattern #9—18½"

Pattern #8—17⅞"

Pattern #10—19"

Pattern #11—24"

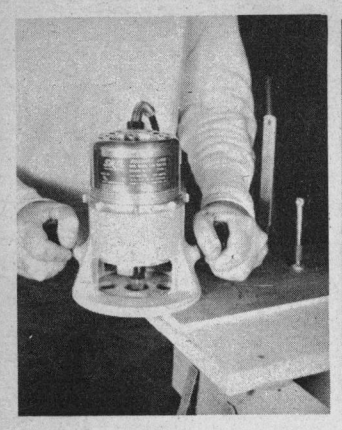

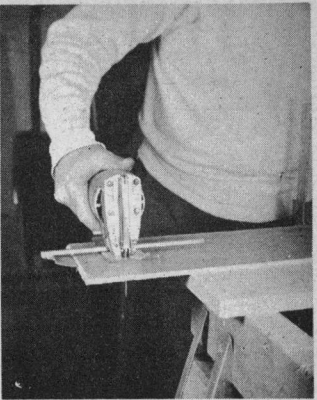

stock and clamp it to a piece of 3/4" scrap. Cut the desired curve in both simultaneously with a sabre saw, following the pattern line carefully. Both pieces stay clamped together; the 3/4" stock is now a template that will guide the router bit.

Now, bring the router into action. With the proper bit chucked in—we used Black & Decker #U2521 to get a rounded edge—the router shapes the edge of the ¼" stock as its noncutting tip follows the guidance to it by the template.

The photo at left, above, shows the router in action.

The rectangular pieces from which the other sides are formed are finished in the same way but no special template is needed. Just clamp the ¼" stock to a straight piece of 3/4" material, with edges flush. Then shape the edge with the router—the left-hand photo at the top of the page actually illustrates this phase of the work. As before, the 3/4" piece guides the cutter along the straight edge of the thinner material.

A sabre saw with a cutting guide attached (photo at top, right) is handy for cutting off a frame piece after the edge has been rounded.

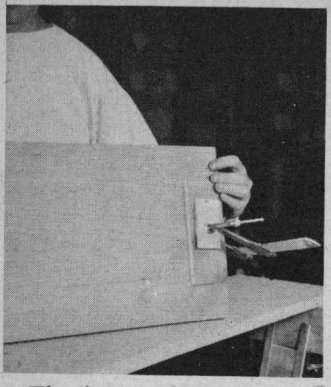

The frame pieces are glued to the door and held tight by clamps until the glue dries, as illustrated at left, above. Do not coat all meeting surfaces with glue. Rather, use a spotting technique, applying only enough glue to assure a good bond. A complete coat of glue may cause some warping of the doors later.

Top right photograph shows the edge of the door. The light wood is 3/4" stock; finger points to the ¼" overlay that makes the design on the face.

The final step in completing the doors is the application of wood tape to conceal the raw edges, as shown at left, below. Apply liberal coat of glue to the meeting surfaces.

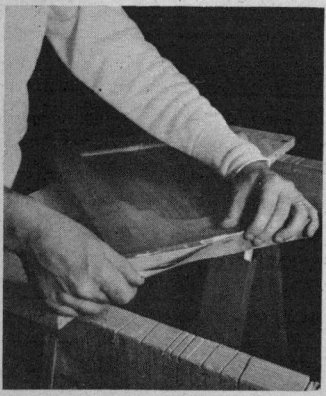

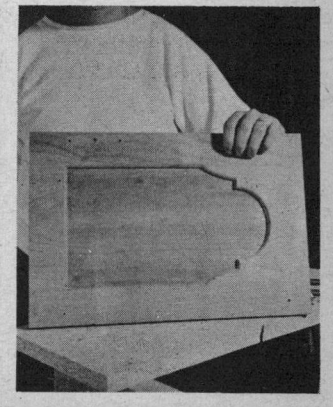

The last photo shows the completed door, ready for hanging. The screw holes have been predrilled, using a hinge as template.

WHAT IT'S CALLED AND WHERE TO BUY IT

Most products mentioned here are sold in hardware and appliance stores and lumber and building supply yards. The manufacturers' names and addresses are listed in the event there are some items your dealer does not carry. Please write to the source listed for further information that you might want about any of these products.

A NEW KITCHEN FOR YOUR FAMILY—page 7—custom kitchens shown on pages 11, 13 and 17 are by *Mutschler Bros. Co., Dept. FH, Nappanee, Ind.* The designs on pages 21, 23, 25 and 27 are by *General Electric*.

A NEW CEILING—page 33—the ceiling in the kitchen shown on page 11 is Woodcrest Cushiontone acoustical tile by *Armstrong Cork Co., Dept. FH, Lancaster, Pa.* Its vinyl acrylic finish is extremely resistant to grease and staining from all common household agents. Installation is shown on pages 35-38. On page 34, top, is shown the installation of Marlite block over an old, cracked ceiling. The plastic-finished hardboard blocks are secured with wallboard adhesive. Both are products of *Marsh Wall Products, Dept. FH, Dover, Ohio.*

The suspended ceiling installation shown on page 42 is of the Alsynite Luminous Ceiling. The installation package comes complete with clips, framing, molding and pre-cut panels, and goes up quickly with simple hand tools. It's by *Alsynite Division of Reichhold Chemicals, Dept. FH, RCI Building, White Plains, N.Y.* Translucent, suspended ceilings are also available from *Owens-Corning Fiberglas, Dept. FH, National Bank Building, Toledo 1, Ohio,* and *Armstrong Cork Co.*

The "exposed beams" shown on pages 39-40 are called Vinylfold, a Gold Bond product of *National Gypsum Co., Dept. FH, Buffalo, N.Y.*

A BRICK WALL—THE EASY WAY—pages 44-45—the realistic-appearing "bricks" used in this kitchen are Miracle Bricks by *Dacor Manufacturing Co., Dept. FH, 72*

Gardner St., Worcester, Mass.

A VINYL WALL—page 46—the wall covering material is Wall Corlon by *Armstrong Cork Co., Dept. FH, Lancaster, Pa.*, which also manufactures the various cements used in its application.

WIPE-CLEAN KITCHEN PANELING—pages 50-51—both the planks and the mural panels are marlite from *Marsh Wall Products, Dept. FH, Dover, Ohio.* Marlite is available through local lumber dealers.

PUT YOUR WALLS TO WORK—page 52—the paneling used is Marlite Woodpanel. The adhesive is Marsh C-350. Both are from *Marsh Wall Products, Dept. FH, Dover, Ohio.*

TILING THE KITCHEN FLOOR—page 58—there are several highly reputable manufacturers of various kinds of floor tiles; one of the leading ones is *Armstrong Cork Company, Dept. FH, Lancaster, Pa.* The installation shown in this article is of Armstrong Excelon vinyl-asbestos tile. The underlayment is Armstrong Temboard. Cement is Armstrong S-700 Brushing Cement.

THE KITCHEN CARPET—page 63—the spot-and stain-resistant carpet of polypropylene olefin fiber is Ozite Town 'N' Terrace. It's by *Ozite Corp., Dept. FH, 7-120 Merchandise Mart, Chicago, Ill.*

EYE-CATCHING IDEA KITCHENS—pages 30-31—the Oriental kitchen seen on page 30 is a model by *Frigidaire Division, Dept. FH, General Motors Corp., Dayton, Ohio 45401*, and features appliances manufactured by that company.

ELECTRICITY IN THE MODERN KITCHEN—page 65—the wall-to-wall ceiling on page 67 is by *Artcrest Products Co., Inc., Dept. FH, 255 W. 79th St., Chicago, Ill.* The Lo-Tone Dome-Lite on page 69 is manufactured by *Wood Conversion Co., Dept. FH, First National Bank Building, St. Paul, Minn. 55101.* The kitchen with the long fluorescent fixture down the middle of the ceiling on the same page is by *Westinghouse*, the hanging fixture over the island work area—page 71—is by *Mutschler Bros. Co., Dept. FH, Nappanee, Ind.*

A KITCHEN VENTILATING SYSTEM—page 72—the no-duct hoods over range and oven shown on pages 72 and 75 (top right) are products of *Nautilus Industries, Inc., Dept. FH, Freeland, Pa.*

LET'S HAVE A BARBECUE—page 76—the fan unit carrying off the heat, smoke and delightful aroma from the turkey roasting on top of page 78 is by *NuTone Inc., Dept. FH, Madison and Red Bank Roads, Cincinnati, Ohio.* The portable unit shown on page 76 is by *The Majestic Company, Inc., Dept. FH, Huntington, Ind.*

KITCHEN CABINETS—page 79—the knocked-down wood assemble-yourself cabinets on page 84-87 are products of the *Morgan Co., Dept. FH, Oshkosh, Wis.* The metal cabinets on pages 88-89 are by *United Metal Cabinet Corp., Dept. FH, Pottsville, Pa.* The lazy susan shelf hardware shown on pages 98-99 is made by *Amerock Corp., Dept. FH, Rockford, Ill.*

COUNTERTOPS—page 105—mosaic tile (pages 112-113) can be purchased at many building supply, department and handicraft stores. An excellent waterproof cement for the tile is available from *Rubber and Asbestos Corp, Dept. FH, 225 Belleville Ave., Bloomfield, N.J.* The vinyl countertop material shown on pages 107-11 is Counter Corlon by *Armstrong Cork Co., Dept. FH, Lancaster, Pa.* Armstrong S-1200 Contact Bond Cement is used to attach moldings, S-127 Cement for applying the material. The fillet strip is Armstrong's Wall Covering Fillet Strip S-15. The hard plastic laminate installations shown on page 114 is by *Formica Corp., Dept. FH, 4614 Spring Grove Ave., Cincinnati, Ohio.* The flexible plastic laminate on pages 115-116 is Conolite, a product of *Wood Conversion Co., Dept. FH, First National Bank Building, St. Paul 1, Minn.*

PLAN A KITCHEN LAUNDRY CENTER—page 124—the excellent planning advice and helpful hints given in this article are courtesy of the Maytag Home Laundry Idea Center. The appliances on page 131, lower photo, are by *Maytag Co., Dept. FH, Newton, Iowa.* The kitchen on page 124 and the laundry center on page 125 are by *Frigidaire Division, Dept. FH, General Motors Corp.,*

Dayton, Ohio. The Stacked Laundry on page 126 is by *Westinghouse*; the laundry-breakfast room combination (page 127) is by *Western Wood Products Association, Dept. FH, Product Information Division, 526 American Bank Building, Portland, Oregon 97205.* The combination laundry, playroom and kitchen on page 128 is from *Marsh Wall Products, Dept. FH, Dover, Ohio.* The workshop kitchen, page 129, is by *Armstrong Cork* and the corner laundry on page 133 again by *Westinghouse.*

A KITCHEN YOU'LL LOVE—page 147—the refrigerator in this kingly kitchen is of the type without a freezer compartment—ideal for a home with a separate freezer unit because it permits storage cabinetry above it at a convenient height. It's by the *Gibson Refrigerator Co., Dept. FH, Greenville, Mich.* The double wall oven, countertop range and dishwasher are all by the *Hotpoint Co., Dept. FH, 5600 W. Taylor St., Chicago 44, Ill.* From *Nutone, Inc., Dept. FH, Madison and Red Bank Rds., Cincinnati 27, Ohio* comes the range hood with built-in fan and light.

At dealers of the *Carrolton Mfg. Co., Dept. FH, Carrolton, Ohio,* you'll find the Carlton stainless steel sink. The single-control faucet is by the *Delta Faucet Corp., Dept. FH, Greensburg, Ind.* The small accessories placed in various convenient locations—the breadboxes, the disappearing pot holder, the pop-up garbage container, the towel racks and assorted spice shelves—are all part of the line of kitchen conveniences by *Washington Steel Products, Inc., Dept. FH, Tacoma 1, Wash.*

Materials used in the kitchen project include Amtico Renaissance vinyl floor tile by the *American Biltrite Rubber Co., Dept. FH, Trenton 2, N.J.* The rich-looking wood used for the cabinets is lumbercore Weldwood plywood by *U.S. Plywood Corp., Dept. FH, 777 Third Ave., New York, N.Y.* The same firm makes the Flexible Wood Trim with which all plywood edges were finished. The antiqued brass hinges and drawer pulls are part of the unusual line of reproductions of antique hardware by the *18th Century Hardware Co., Dept. FH, 319 E. Main St., Ligonier, Pa.* The adjustable shelf hardware is by *Standard-Keil Mfg. Co., Inc., Dept. FH, 2581 Atlantic Ave., Brooklyn, N.Y.* Drawer slides are by *Washington Steel Products.*